The SHORTSTOP

The SHORTSTOP

Baseball
Behind The Seams

ROB TRUCKS

CINCINNATI, OHIO

The SHORTSTOP
Baseball Behind the Seams

EMMIS BOOKS
1700 Madison Road
Cincinnati, Ohio 45206
www.emmisbooks.com

Library of Congress Control Number: 2005937416
ISBN 1-57860-262-9

Edited by Jack Heffron
Cover and interior design by Stephen Sullivan
Interior production by Angela Wilcox

Cover photo STAN HONDA/AFP/Getty Images
Back cover image by Ezra Shaw/Getty Images Sport/Getty Images

DEDICATION

For Freddie Patek, Tim Foli, and Jay Bell

And for Karan, always for Karan

ACKNOWLEDGMENTS

Thanks, of course, to all the shortstops who so generously provided time, conversation, and insight.

Thanks also to Jack Heffron and the fine folks at Emmis Books. Thanks to Eric Phillips and Katie Kirby of the Chicago White Sox, Jay Alves of the Colorado Rockies, and Greg Casterioto of the Philadelphia Phillies, as well as a support system including but not limited to Will Blythe, Tony Brusate, Bill Dessoffy, Will Kimbrough, Emilie Marvosa, John Marvosa, Laurie Mundy, Marilyn Rinaldo, Beth Shea, Michael Smith, Linda Trucks, Steve Trucks, and Wayne Trucks.

A special thanks to Sean Forman and his wonderful Web site http://www.baseball-reference.com for research assistance above and beyond the call of duty.

TABLE OF CONTENTS

OZZIE SMITH

1ST

Portrait of the Shortstop as an Athlete

B y definition, every major leaguer is an athlete. And a professional athlete at that. But despite constitutional suggestions regarding the status of men, not all athletes are created equal. (I could name a few 1970s-era relief pitchers who would have difficulty extricating themselves from a fire if they lived above, say, the first floor.)

Take a drive to your local Little League field—the ballpark where eight, nine, and ten year olds experience the joys of winning, the agony of being left on the bench, and the utter boredom of being placed in the outfield. (A certain right fielder from my Little League playing days was nicknamed Clover because he spent all of his defensive time looking for four-leaf clovers in the outfield grass.) Don't bother watching the game. Look just to the left of second base. There he is. The shortstop.

There's a better-than-even chance you've just found the best overall athlete on the team.

Why? Because the preponderance of balls put into Little League play will find their way to the shortstop.

The SHORTSTOP

Outside of the pitcher's delivery from the mound and the catcher's attempted receipt of a near astronomical number of balls, especially among the youngest participants, the shortstop will be more active than any other player on the field.

The shortstop, not unlike the center fielder in the outfield behind him, will take charge in nearly every infield situation. He will field ground balls, chase pop-ups. He will also be involved in double plays, stolen base attempts. And, outside of the third baseman, he has the longest throw on the field (but not by much if the pair are positioned correctly).

The shortstop is undeniably a skill position and, because of the required athleticism, more likely born than made. And because of the demands of the job, if the best athlete on the Little League field fails to automatically gravitate toward shortstop on his own, often his coach will assist the magnetic pull emanating from the middle infield.

A Little League shortstop must be quick, possess a strong arm, and throw right-handed. There is also, of course, that seemingly unquantifiable matter of range. Range can, in fact, be measured (don't touch that dial), but not to any firm, scientific accuracy. For the meantime, think of range as the ability to personify a video game system's joystick. Range is the ability to move in any and all directions smoothly and efficiently. So it makes sense that the best athlete on the Little League field will find himself at the shortstop position.

Getty Images

DICK GROAT

Though many major league shortstops have been blessed with a wealth and variety of athletic talent, perhaps no man, in terms of pure athleticism, comes to mind more readily than Dick Groat.

Groat, of course, was named the National League's Most Valuable Player in 1960, the year that his Pittsburgh Pirates went on to defeat the New York Yankees four games to three in the World Series thanks to a ninth inning home run in game seven by Groat's double-play partner, Bill Mazeroski.

But before Groat reached the major leagues he was a two-sport standout at Duke University. In both 1951 and 1952 (before Duke was a member of the Atlantic Coast Conference) Dick Groat was the Southern Con-

13

ference Basketball Tournament MVP. In both 1951 and 1952 Dick Groat was the Southern Conference Basketball Player of the Year. In 1952 Groat was the first basketball player in Duke history to be selected as a first-team All-American. At season's end Groat was the first round draft pick of the NBA's Fort Wayne Pistons.

And yet after a single, well-traveled season (the Pistons chartered a plane to ferry Groat to and from his rookie season games and the remainder of his Duke classes), Groat gave up his professional basketball career to concentrate on baseball.

"I regret that I didn't have the opportunity to play at least both sports for two or three years," Groat says, "but Mr. Rickey would not buy it, and I'm not sure that Mr. Rickey wasn't right."

Mr. Rickey, of course, is Branch Rickey, an off-the-field "visionary" who experienced but a "mediocre career as a player and a manager" according to the Baseball Hall of Fame's web site. As a player Mr. Rickey set a major league record for stolen bases allowed when the Yankees swiped 13 in a single game with Rickey as catcher. As a manager Mr. Rickey captained just three winning campaigns in ten seasons, and finished with a career winning percentage of .473.

But as a general manager, among other feats, Mr. Rickey created the uniquely innovative St. Louis Cardinals' farm system, signed Jackie Robinson for the Brooklyn Dodgers, and, as the president of the Pittsburgh Pirates, stole Roberto Clemente away from the Dodgers in baseball's post-season draft.

Groat considers Mr. Rickey "one of the finest minds in the history of baseball." According to Groat, when Mr. Rickey wanted to try out an infielder, "he always worked them out at shortstop. He always felt that if he had a shortstop he had a third baseman, a second baseman, and a first baseman. If he could play shortstop he could play anywhere."

As with so many other of his innovations, baseball general managers have followed Mr. Rickey's lead ever since.

Baseball's first amateur draft took place in June of 1965. Before that date, professional organizations signed free agents at will, based on scouting and who got there first (it was Mr. Rickey's Cardinals who signed seemingly any American male who could throw a baseball and piled them into the league's largest minor league system, allowing a certain Draconian "survival of the fittest" philosophy rule from there).

Rick Monday, an outfielder from Arizona State University, was the first overall pick. Monday would reach the majors the following year with the Kansas City Athletics, his first of 19 consecutive seasons in the big leagues.

But in the twenty picks made in the first round of the first draft, three shortstops—Alex Barrett, a high schooler out of California, John Wyatt, another high schooler from California (notice a trend here?), and Eddie Leon from the University of Arizona—were chosen. Of the three, only Leon made it all the way to the majors.

In that first draft, seven pitchers were selected in the first round, leaving 13 position players. Given that there are eight defensive positions not played on a ten-inch high mound, one out of every eight selections should be a shortstop in order to hold to an average. And yet in this first draft three picks out of 13 were shortstops, or right at 23 percent, nearly double the expected average of 12½ percent.

Indeed, it appears Mr. Rickey's theory that a good shortstop can play any position has been passed down.

In 1966 Steve Chilcott, a high school catcher from California, was taken by the Mets as the first overall pick of the draft. Chilcott never made it to the majors. Of the eleven position players taken, three were shortstops. Two were university players, from Indiana and California. The third was a high school player by the name of Richie Hebner. Taken at number fifteen by the Pittsburgh Pirates, Hebner, a gravedigger in the off-season, went on to play in over 1900 major league ballgames, the majority at third base. He played exactly zero games at shortstop.

In 1967, fourteen position players were taken in the first twenty picks. The most notable was Bobby Grich, the 19th selection overall, who, though brought up as a shortstop in 1970, had transitioned to second base by 1973 where he played in over 1700 major league contests. Grich would be selected six times as an American League All-Star.

In 1968: four shortstops, or 25 percent of the sixteen position players taken in the first round. This includes the number one overall pick, Tim Foli, who actually played over 80 percent of his major league games at short.

In 1969 the draft expanded to 24 four picks per round. And a full third of position players taken in the first round, six out of eighteen, were selected as shortstops. Alan Bannister, a high schooler out of (you guessed it) California, was taken at number five but refused to sign (he was later drafted by the Phillies and played 167 major league games at short, but also played almost 400 in the outfield and over 250 at second). Don "Full Pack" Stanhouse, selected as both a pitcher and a shortstop at number nine, would receive his greatest notoriety as Baltimore's anxiety-inducing closer in 1978 and 1979. Future Gold Glove winner Roger Metzger was taken by the Cubs at number 16, future National League utility infielder Mike Phillips at number 18, and, most surprising of all, at least as a shortstop pick (since at least one Web site has nominated him for the "slowest, fattest centerfielder ever"), future Milwaukee Brewers slugger Gorman Thomas.

In 1970, six out of fifteen position players selected in the first round were shortstops.

The draft in 1971 was remarkable for two reasons. First, a record high eight of 12 positions players select-ed—yes, a credulity-threatening 67 percent, or two out of every three position players—in the first round listed shortstop as their primary position. Two of those eight—specifically the Expos' pick at number four, Con-dredge Holloway, and the Reds' selection at number twenty-four, Mike Miley—became starting quarterbacks in the Southeastern Conference.

Holloway not only was a starting shortstop at the University of Tennessee but played well enough to be named to the university's Baseball Hall of Fame. However, it was on the football field that Holloway received his greatest acclaim. He was named a football All-American in 1973 and, after graduating from UT, he went on to play in the Canadian Football League. Nicknamed "The Artful Dodger" for his scrambling ability, Holloway won the league MVP award in 1982 as the quarterback for the Toronto Argonauts. He was inducted into the Canadian Football Hall of Fame, had his jersey retired by the Argonauts, and was named to the Canadian Football League's 125th Anniversary Team.

Miley also bypassed his first chance at pro ball to attend LSU. As a quarterback, Miley led the Tigers to an Orange Bowl victory. In 1974 he was once again a first round selection (the only shortstop to be selected in the first round twice). Miley played part of two seasons with the California Angels before passing away on January 6, 1977, following an off-season car accident in Baton Rouge.

And while 1971 might stand as a singular testament to both the importance of the position as well as the athletic versatility of those who play shortstop, it would, by no means, be the final example of either.

Shortstops would be the number one overall pick of the 1974 draft (Bill Almon), 1982 (Shawon Dunston), 1990 (Chipper Jones), 1993 (Alex Rodriguez) as well as each of the past two years, 2004 (Matt Bush) and 2005

(Justin Upton). While Almon, Dunston, and Rodriguez (thus far) have played the majority of their games at short, fewer than 50 of Chipper Jones's 1651 appearances to date have been at shortstop.

In 1994 another future LSU quarterback, Josh Booty, was drafted by the Florida Marlins. Booty would appear in 13 games for the Marlins, including 12 appearances at third base, before returning to college to play football. He was drafted by the Seattle Seahawks in the 6th round of the 2001 NFL draft.

In 1972, four future major league fixtures were all drafted as shortstops. Rick Manning would play 13 major league seasons in the outfield, Jamie Quirk would play 18 seasons with the majority of his appearances at catcher, Jerry Manuel would only play five seasons, primarily as a second baseman, but would manage the Chicago White Sox for six seasons, and former shortstop Chet Lemon would play in 1988 games over 16 major league seasons with Chicago and Detroit without a single appearance at short.

Already mentioned is the 1993 first overall selection of Alex Rodriguez by Seattle. The year before, the Yankees selected Derek Jeter. The year after, the Red Sox picked Nomar Garciaparra (and if this book had been written three seasons ago, or even if Garciaparra had managed to stay with the Red Sox through their World Series win, you can believe we'd be adding at least a couple more paragraphs on how these three selections represent the changing face of the shortstop. Oh Nomar, we hardly knew ye).

The Milwaukee Brewers would strike pay dirt with the third overall pick in both 1973 and 1977. Their 1973 selection, Robin Yount, would play in over 2850 big league games, just over half of those games at shortstop, and collect two American League MVP awards in his 20 seasons. In 1999 Yount would be inducted into the Baseball Hall of Fame. Paul Molitor, drafted four years after Yount, would play 21 years, 15 of them with the Brewers. A seven-time All-Star, Molitor would play but 57 games at shortstop, none after 1982. In 2004 he would be the first designated hitter elected to the Hall of Fame.

In 1986 both future third baseman Matt Williams and future outfielder Gary Sheffield would be first round selections at shortstop. Even more of an imagination stretch would take place with the 1978 selection of future first baseman Nick Esasky, future outfielder Cory Snyder in 1984, future first baseman Dmitri Young in 1991 and future catcher Michael Barrett in 1995. All stand at least 6'2" with only Snyder weighing less than 200 pounds. None of the four, in fact, fit the pre-Ripken stereotype of the shortstop build and in hindsight there's little surprise in the movement of any of the four.

And why do so many one-time shortstops—not just Esasky, Snyder, Young, and Barrett, but Chipper Jones and Paul Molitor and Richie Hebner and Gorman Thomas and Gary Sheffield and Jamie Quirk and Bobby Grich—find new positions? Of course, there might be a backlog at the position within the organization. Bill Almon, a number one overall draft pick, found himself a utility player with the arrival of Ozzie Smith in San

Diego. But a shortstop needs more range than your average third baseman. A shortstop needs a stronger throwing arm than your average second baseman. And because of his positioning in the middle of the field, a major league shortstop will suffer more wear and tear on his body than any other position besides catcher.

Just as Johnny Bench played significantly more games at both third and first than catcher in the last three years of his career, and just as Mike Piazza will assuredly move to the American League where he can play every day as a designated hitter, so too do shortstops move. Though not always so visibly.

In the pre-Ripken era shortstops were placed in the lineup for their defense, and often their defense alone. Mark Belanger, Ripken's predecessor in Baltimore, played 18 major league seasons on four American League pennant winners and collected eight Gold Glove Awards, yet only managed a career batting average of .228. When Belanger could no longer play shortstop he retired. There was no other position available.

But Ernie Banks' bat was certainly strong enough to find another spot in the lineup when the strain of serving as an everyday shortstop began to take its toll. Banks won the National League MVP award in 1958 and 1959 and the Gold Glove in 1960, but he didn't play a game at short after the 1961 season. And "Mr. Cub" didn't retire until after the 1971 season.

Robin Yount was a shortstop his first eleven years, an outfielder his last nine. Even the great Honus Wagner, after 20 years as a big league shortstop, played his final season at first base.

In fact, only the truly mystifying Luke Appling, inducted into the Hall of Fame in 1964, seems to have put the whammy on Father Time. After splitting duties between third and short the previous year, in 1949, at the age of 42, Appling returned as the White Sox' everyday shortstop and performed more than adequately. Not only did Appling manage a .301 batting average in 141 games, he committed but 26 errors at short. Not Mike Bordick numbers to be sure, but it was his lowest error total in eleven seasons.

Yea verily, I say unto you, a good shortstop is hard to find. But not for lack of looking.

In the first thirty-five years of baseball's amateur draft, 514 position players have been selected in the first round. And though the shortstop comprises a mere $12\frac{1}{2}$ percent of defensive positions, out of those 514 players 144 shortstops have been selected. Put another way, 28 percent of all position players selected in the first round have been shortstops at the time of the draft, more than double the statistical defensive need.

Of these 144 selected shortstops, an even hundred have seen their careers reach all the way to the major leagues, and yet only 41 of those hundred played in the majors with shortstop as their primary position. Of the 100 former shortstops drafted in the first round of baseball's amateur draft who reached the majors, 21 played in the outfield, 16 at third, 14 at second and two each at catcher, first, DH, and pitcher.

To play shortstop requires both skill and athleticism

National Baseball Hall of Fame Library/Major League Baseball/Getty Images

LUKE APPLING

in ample amounts, as well as a durability rarely challenged on the diamond. But as Branch Rickey said, find a good shortstop and you can play him anywhere.

2ND

In the Beginning

When We Were Little Boys

I had a real good arm, so in Little League I played short and I pitched. After Little League, obviously, I just started focusing on shortstop. I think I was better than anybody on the team, but not like, God, who's that out there?

— *Larry Bowa*

Originally I was a catcher, the first time I ever played organized baseball, probably due to the fact that they didn't have a catcher and I was the only one pretty much willing to do it. And so they threw me behind there. I didn't really didn't care where I was playing. I was happy just to be on the field. I caught for two years and then, once I moved to short, I stayed there all the way up until my freshman year in college. Played two years at third, and then moved back to short and I've been there since then.

— *Khalil Greene*

KHALIL GREENE

Rob Leiter/Major League Baseball/Getty Images

I was eight when I started playing organized baseball with A & T Travel in the Oakland Babe Ruth League. I think I first played as a third baseman. They had an older guy who been there the year before at shortstop, Rob Sasser, who ended up playing with the Detroit Tigers. I know he had a cup of coffee with the big league squad, but he was pretty much a minor leaguer. And when he went to the next level, then I moved to shortstop.

— *Jimmy Rollins*

From day one I was a third baseman. I went to Mississippi State, and out of Mississippi State I signed with the White Sox organization and played my first year in A ball in Muskegon, Michigan. Third basemen have to be able, in most cases, to hit the ball harder than I could hit it. Hit home runs and knock in runs. But I had good hands, so they wanted to turn me into a shortstop. I played shortstop at Memphis, and it was a little difficult because I had never played it, and not knocking the manager we had, but in those days they didn't talk to you about how to play. I mean, you just went out and played.

— *Alex Grammas*

Jack McKeon, the manager of the Florida Marlins, we grew up together and went to the same high school and grade school in South Amboy, New Jersey. We started by playing for his dad's team. His dad had the McKeon's Boys' Club team, and we all played for it. In fact, we used to kid that we had the first indoor stadium because when it rained his dad would take the cars out of the garage and we'd hit in his garage all the time. And that's how we got started, but with me it was a little different. I never played in the infield. I was always an outfielder. Up to the time I came to Pittsburgh I'd never played at all in the infield. I was always a center fielder. My brother John was the infielder, and he played shortstop and third base most of the time. There was no Little League when we played so when we were in the various leagues and the semi-pro teams that we played for I was always the center fielder and John was either the third baseman or the shortstop.

— *Eddie O'Brien*

I just signed up one day and they just handed you a T-shirt and a cap. They didn't have uniforms back then. You had a pair of jeans. And I was out in left field. I felt like a lost pup. I kind of walked into a situation where teams had already been picked. I think that's the way Little Leagues are run. There's always people out there saying, I want this guy, this guy, this guy, and I was kind of new in the neighborhood and walked into this area and I wanted to play and that's where they stuck me. You kind of felt like a fish out of water but you just went along and did what you had to do. You've got the support of your family and encouragement and you just kind of keep going.

— *Roger Metzger*

I played shortstop and pitcher. I had such a good arm.

That's one of the things that I think people look for when you're starting out in Little League is they look for the kid who's got the best arm, and they'll either put him on the mound or put him usually at shortstop. Because I had such a good arm that's where I ended up.

— *Bobby Bonner*

I knew baseball since I was in the first grade. I had a brother. We used to play against each other in stopper-ball, and he'd be the Yankees and I'd be the Red Sox. And if Billy Goodman came up, I'd hit first, left-handed like Billy Goodman. And second was Bobby Doerr, I'd bat right-handed. Third was Ted Williams, I'd bat left-handed. I wish I'd have kept going.

— *Don Buddin*

I played on a team that went to the Little League World Series in 1962, and I played shortstop for the fifteen games, from the first game up until the last game of the Little League World Series. And then my four years of high school I was a shortstop.

I had an older brother who was a shortstop in high school and so I kind of just migrated towards that position. Then I had a cousin who was a decent shortstop and I looked up to those guys as a kid.

— *Larvell Blanks*

As a player I started right out as a shortstop, although my dad was my Little League coach and he was a firm believer in everybody knowing all nine positions. But I was a shortstop in Little League and that's pretty much all I played, besides a little pitching here and there, right into my professional career.

— *Bill Almon*

I was an infielder all my life. I started out at second base. I didn't play Little League or anything like that, just pick-up baseball when we were growing up, and then in high school I started at second base and went to American Legion that summer and the shortstop went on vacation and I moved to shortstop and I never left shortstop from that point on.

— *Dick Groat*

I started in the outfield. I was a center fielder because I could run a little bit and was pretty good at judging balls. I became a shortstop probably in high school. I think that's when I first became a shortstop.

— *Paul Zuvella*

What I Want to Do When I Grow Up
I did dream about it. That's all I wanted to do, since I was a Little Leaguer, but obviously not making the high school team sort of derailed those dreams. And then I sort of conjured them up again when I played American Legion and did good. And then obviously going to Sacramento—it was City College at the time, which was a perennial baseball powerhouse in junior college—and I made that team and played two years, made all-conference. The whole time I watched TV, and I watched Luis

Aparicio and Nellie Fox who were relatively small players, and I figured, If those guys can do it, why can't I do it? It was my life, at that time, and it's still my life.

— *Larry Bowa*

My dad wasn't home very much. He worked in the oil fields, and I didn't have a brother to play with, so I just practiced. I'd get a tennis ball and throw it up against the garage door and just field two hops, three hops, and I'd make up games where I played defense. You've just got to practice. That's it. In the summertime I'd go to the ball field at nine o'clock in the morning and come home at five-thirty or six. I just played, played, played. I dreamed of being a major leaguer, never even thinking it would happen.

— *Daryl Spencer*

Well, it sounds really egotistical when I tell you this. When I was nine years old I told my big sister I was going to be an All-American basketball player, I was going to be an All-American baseball player, I was going to play in the NBA, I was going to play with the Pirates and I was never going to play minor league baseball.

— *Dick Groat*

I wanted it more than anybody you could even think of. I used to bounce the tennis ball against the garage every day. I would create ways to do things by myself when my dad wasn't around. I really believe that I developed soft hands by doing these drills every day. I grew up in the

31

Sacramento area, and I wanted to play winter ball. So instead of looking for an adult, I went to the City of Sacramento Recreation Department. I got all the forms. I was the manager and player, and I got all my friends to play in winter league. I'd make the lineups, and I'd manage a team as I played, just so we could play in the winter. It was more of a love for me than anything else. I mean, I loved the game so much. I wanted to play it so bad.
— *Mike Fischlin*

If We Could Be Heroes
I never had a hero. I always used to watch the ones that do a little better than anybody else to see what they do to learn from them. Actually I can't understand why people want my autograph. I was in there for a cup of coffee. I got hit in the eye with the ball and that was the end of my career, and I probably get at least two letters every month. At least. They want my autograph. But I do it because the people, that's their thing. It was never my thing. I don't ever remember getting an autograph, not one time, because, to me, people are individuals. You could have the greatest baseball player in the world but he's really a jerk. Who cares? Who wants it? Now say you have a guy who's an average baseball player but just a wonderful individual, spiritually a good guy. I'd much rather be with that guy.
— *Jack Kubiszyn*

My dad played, as high as Triple A. Managed in the minor leagues. He was like a minor league rat, I guess

32

you might want to say. He taught me about never quitting, fight to the last out. If you're ever frustrated in the batter's box or in the field, don't show it. Believe in yourself, no matter what the odds are. If you're 0 for 25, that 26th time up you've got to believe you're going to get a hit. So I try to live by that philosophy.

— *Larry Bowa*

Larry Bowa was someone I really followed because he was from my hometown. I remember the first time I got to the big leagues Larry came over and congratulated me, gave me one of his gloves. That always had some impact to me. You know, he's a feisty, competitive guy, and was somebody I idolized because the guy was an overachiever. Without a doubt. I mean, that guy made himself a player, and look what he did with his career. It's unbelievable. He was somebody that probably gave me motivation like, if he can do it, I can do it.

— *Mike Fischlin*

I have an uncle who played service baseball back during the Korean War, and he played in these summer leagues in the Texas hill country. He was a very gifted athlete. And I used to go to ballgames with him. I was just a little guy, and so I was always out there shagging balls and hanging around the ballpark. So you kind of got familiar with what a real fly ball looks like, balls that an adult's hitting, and he always made me stay in the outfield because that's the safest place to be when you're four and five years old, so you don't get killed. I loved to

go those games. I was a batboy and before the games you got to hang out in the outfield and catch fly balls, and after the game when everybody else was off the field the kids would go out there and play baseball, so it was kind of just part of the development. To tell you the truth, my uncle was kind of my mentor. He played baseball, and he would encourage me and work with me. I can always remember, he said, "If you don't throw hard, you don't play." He always told me, "If you can't hurt my hand you're not throwing hard enough." Well, obviously, I never threw hard enough to hurt his hand but I always tried.
— *Roger Metzger*

I liked so many different players, and I kind of appreciated just little things a lot of different guys did. At the time Canseco and Bonds were probably two of my favorite players—Canseco because he was so prominent on the scene at that time and Bonds just for the fact that I was born in Pittsburgh and always liked the Pirates and he was the guy for them at that time when I was kind of getting into it.
— *Khalil Greene*

My favorite player was Ricky Henderson. One, he was fast. Speed always attracts an athlete. If somebody's fast, that's who you pay attention to. Two, he wasn't the biggest guy out there, but he sure did put on a show. Showmanship in sports—well, in baseball—I think it's sometimes overlooked because they see it as showing up somebody, but, no, it's showmanship. People pay to see the game, and they want to be entertained. Running to your spot, hitting and running, that doesn't do it. I watched Ozzie Smith. I watched Cal Ripken Jr., and I watched Mike Bordick because he was in Oakland. You naturally rotate to guys playing your position, but I didn't pay a quarter as much attention to them as I did to Ricky.

I met him my rookie year or second year. He was in San Diego, whichever year that was, in the weight room lifting weights, and I looked at the lineup, and I thought, Ricky's not playing today, so maybe he's in the weight room lifting. So I just walk in, and there he is hitting some curls with the dumbbell. I walk right over to the dumbbell bar, right next to him, start lifting, saying, "What's up?" He says, "What's up, Jimmy?" I'm like— Man, he knows my name. I said, "I watched you ever since I was eight years old. You were my favorite player." He started laughing and smiling. Like, I'm from Oakland. He went to Oakland Tech. My dad went to Mackey. Ya'll played against each other. James Rollins. I remember him. Yeah, okay, okay. It's just so funny that I was thinking that he was going to be lifting weights. I don't know why I thought that, but it worked.

— *Jimmy Rollins*

I grew up in Wichita, Kansas. I still live here, and the only team that we could follow was the Cardinals, and Marty Marion was my idol. I'm talking about the 40s and radio. We never had TV, so I never saw him. I saw maybe a picture in the paper, but I never saw any actual plays

John Marvosa

JIMMY ROLLINS

that Marty Marion made, so it would be hard for me to describe him. He just was a tall shortstop, and I liked shortstops. We didn't follow the Yankees or the Cubs or anybody else, because the Cardinals rebroadcast their games here in Wichita, and everybody was a Cardinals fan.

— Daryl Spencer

I'm in a small town of about five hundred people in South Carolina and the closest team to us would be the Atlanta Braves. The Braves weren't any good, and they weren't on TV like they are now. I kind of followed the

Cincinnati Reds. They had Concepcion and Joe Morgan and Johnny Bench and those guys. I remember Cesar Geronimo. That name just stuck with me. I followed the Cincinnati Reds and Concepcion, because I played short-stop. I always kind of admired him.

— *Bill Spiers*

Alvin Dark has always been my idol. First of all he taught me so much about the hit and run. And to give you some idea what a class gentleman he is, I was a rookie, right out of college, and we were playing the Giants at Forbes Field, and I had marks all up and down my ankles, every place, and he got to second base, and he said to me, "Young man, when the game's over I want to see you in the tunnel after the game." We went to second base and he worked with me on the double play. Now he's playing with the Giants and he taught me so much. I'll never ever forget all the help Alvin Dark was to me over my career. He helped me so much with hit-and-run situations, the counts that we should use and why we used them and so forth, and it worked out extremely well for me. My entire career I hit and run on my own, picked my pitches, and it was based on the things that Alvin Dark taught me. He's a first-class man in every possible way.

— *Dick Groat*

Getting There
Started playing Legion Ball in the summer. Played in the summer league. The junior college coach saw me play

37

in the summer league and asked me to come out and basically I said to him if I couldn't make my high school team, how am I going to make the junior college team? And he said, "Well, I don't care how big you are." He said, "I think you can play." So I went out and played two years of junior college, the second year made all-conference, and they had a draft and everything, and I went through the draft, didn't get drafted, and the Phillies offered me a contract to go play A ball in Spartanburg, South Carolina. I jumped at the opportunity, just an opportunity to go play.

— *Larry Bowa*

Back then the rules were a little different. The scouts weren't supposed to talk to you. My college coach was very protective, in a positive way, and he literally would run them off. But they only wanted to know if I interested in playing. After the college season was over, I got a few calls, and they said, "What do you want to do?" And I said, "I'm going to Liberal to play summer ball again." So I went up there and we really hadn't started our season because it didn't kick off until the middle of June, and I think the draft was June 6th or 7th. That was a program where the guys worked during the season. You worked at a job because you couldn't get paid, and so I was at my job and my boss came in and goes, "Did you hear you've been drafted by the Chicago Cubs?" And I go, "Wow. Cool." Evidently one of the directors from the Liberal team told the guy I needed to call Holland, the general manager of the Cubs. I can't remember his first name. Really nice man. So I called, and he said, "I want you to know that you've been drafted by the Chicago Cubs, and you were the 16th pick." And I thought it was the 16th round, but come to find out it was the first round and the 16th pick. I packed my bags and went home, talked to my coaches, and got some input on what I should do. Of course, your college coach doesn't want you to leave, but he said, "You've got to do what you've got to do." I went from college to Triple A in a matter of three weeks.

— *Roger Metzger*

Bing Crosby contacted us in Seattle, while we were playing for Seattle [University] in our junior year, and said he wanted to talk to us—when we finished would we be interested? He had minority ownership in the Pirates. In fact, I've got letters from him here and so forth. He kept in contact with us all during our junior and senior year, and in those days you could sign with anybody. It's not like today where you're drafted.

And so we did go back to Pittsburgh, worked out in the summer. You'd just go work out with the team, and we met Branch Rickey then. And so we knew Rickey from that couple of meetings and of course the five or six, seven occasions we met with Bing Crosby. Ed McCarrick, the Pittsburgh scout, was the one that signed us. In our senior year we went to the NCAA tournament and won two games and lost the third game and came back to Seattle and then decided we were going to sign with Pittsburgh. One of the reasons we signed is Rickey and

Crosby had convinced us that we were going to get a chance to play. They said, "It's not like going to a team, even though as bonus players you'd sit there for two years and not play much. You're going to get some playing time in." That was one of the key things, that we were going to get a chance to play.

— *Eddie O'Brien*

I was drafted out of high school as a pitcher by the Montreal Expos in the 10th round in 1974, but I did not want to sign as a pitcher. I wanted to play shortstop. I had over 30 college scholarships to pitch around the nation, but the only college that said I could play shortstop every day was Texas A & M University. So I signed with Texas A & M with a scholarship and played shortstop for them for four years. In those years it was very difficult for me to sit still. I was very antsy. I wanted to be in the middle of things. I didn't want to be called on every four or five games, and if you're having a bad game within the first ten minutes of your outing you don't even get to pitch, and then you have to wait another five days. I wanted to be right in the middle of things all the time.

— *Bobby Bonner*

I didn't make my high school team as a sophomore and my junior year I broke an elbow or something in a pickup basketball game. But when I was a senior, our team won the state championship here in Kansas, and I think I led the team with a .400 average. I also led the team in

RBIs. But I never had a scout talk to me about playing pro ball, so I stayed around Wichita in '47 and '48 and played semi-pro baseball. Never hit a home run. But the manager of that team also happened to be the guy that taught me how to play percentage ball in Little League. And in 1949 he went to Pauls Valley, Oklahoma, as the manager, and he took five of us kids from Wichita. Like I say, I never talked to a scout or anybody. I went down to Pauls Valley, and that was my first year in pro baseball, 1949, and I think I made $150 a month.

— *Daryl Spencer*

I was drafted in June in the free agent draft, and a week or two weeks later Al Lammachia signed me. He signed a bunch of guys out of south Texas. I drove from there to Shreveport. I signed immediately. I had no doubts. I just went to play baseball. It was a new career for me. I graduated from high school in '69, that May 23rd, and June 12th I was on my way to Shreveport.

— *Larvell Blanks*

Actually, getting drafted by Atlanta was a good thing for me because they didn't really have a lot in the way of middle infielders at the time if I remember right. I think that's why I was able to move up pretty quickly through the minor leagues. I mean, my first full year I was in Double A, and then I spent one year there, and then I was in Triple A, and by the end of that year I was in the big leagues.

— *Paul Zuvella*

We had an idea of where the range should be for the bonus, and I wanted to play. It was pretty painless. We did it pretty quickly. The only thing that I really insisted on, that we really put a high value on, was that I get a major league contract when I signed. They balked at first and then they gave in. But it wasn't a hard fight by any means.

— *Bill Almon*

Mr. Rickey gave me the opportunity. I knew I had to go into the Army. I was going to graduate from college, and had the opportunity to play in the NBA. I wanted to play in the major leagues before I went in the service, and I thought I was intelligent enough that if I couldn't make it in the major leagues I would know enough to go back to the minor leagues later. If I go to the minor leagues, I don't know whether I can play major league baseball yet. And I was fortunate enough that he gave me the opportunity to start two days after I signed, and I led the Pirates in hitting. I came back from the College World Series. That was on Sunday night. I signed Monday night, joined the Pirates on Tuesday, watched the game on Tuesday, pinch-hit on Wednesday, and started on Thursday and played every game the rest of the season. Went back to Duke to finish up on my diploma. I had a very light schedule, and the Pistons got a private plane to fly me from Durham to wherever the Pistons were playing. I've always been, and know now at age 74, I was a much better basketball player than baseball player.

— *Dick Groat*

Bonus Money

It was $2,000. But at that time bonus babies were making big money. It could've been $1,000, it could've been $500. I would've signed just to get the opportunity. And I knew going in. My dad prepped me. He said, "This is a tough business. Not only do you have to be good, you have to be at the right place at the right time. You've got to be lucky." He basically laid down all the parameters of why it won't work, because he didn't want me to be disappointed. I said, "All I want is an opportunity." And I went there, and I played A ball, Double A, and Triple A in three years, then I was in the big leagues.

— *Larry Bowa*

It was $25,000 and $6,000 to play the first year. If you got $25,000 you were a bonus player and had to remain with the team for two years. I think what they did is they increased the number of players you could carry from 25 to 27. The minimum wage was $4,000 in those days.

— *Eddie O'Brien*

The Minors

They came to my house, signed me, gave me a plane ticket, and the next day I was on my way to Atlanta where the Cubs were playing, and I got to work out with the team there. I worked that day, and then the next morning I was on a plane going to the Seattle/Tacoma Airport. That's where the Triple A team was, and so I'm thinking, Okay, this is like a cup of coffee. They're going to test me, and I'm going to stay here for a week or two, and then I'll go to Double A, maybe Class A. Whitey Lockman was my first manager, and he calls me in and says, "The game's no different here than anywhere else. You catch it, you throw it, and you hit it. I got to the big leagues when I was 19. There's no reason you can't do it." And I said, "Okay." He said, "By the way, we're leaving tomorrow on a road trip to Hawaii." So I was in the big leagues then. But the thing that flipped me was I went out and put my uniform on and got out on the field as fast as I could, and I'm out taking ground balls. The catcher, Randy Bobb, was looking at the lineup, and he yells out, "Hey, the rook's in the lineup." Whitey stuck me in there and gave me about a week of playing time, and then he could tell I was a little rusty and intimidated, and he took me out. He never said a lot, but he told me, "Look, I'm not sitting you out because I don't think you can play. You just need to catch your breath." Tacoma was fighting for the PCL championship. So he took me out for a couple of games and put me back in, and I played the rest of the season. He had a lot of confidence in me.

— *Roger Metzger*

I went to spring training in '83 happy as can be because Earl's gone. I knew that they're moving Ripken to short. I knew I'm out of a job, but I also had been playing second, third, outfield. I'm a utility man. I'm a team player. I'm an Oriole. So I go in '83 to spring training. I play. I spot play. I hit about .350. I played pretty good at second, third, wherever they want me, and then Joe

Altobelli calls me in the office the last day of spring training and says, "Bobby, we're going to send you down to the minor leagues." And I go, "Okay, I figured that." Ripken's the shortstop. He says, "Do you want to know why?" And I'm thinking, well, sure. And he said these words to me, and I'll never forget them. He said, "You're taking this Jesus thing too far. You have to leave your Bible in church. You're making everybody nervous. Nobody wants to be around you." I said, "Joe, what do you mean?" He said, "You've got to leave Jesus in the church." And I said, "Jesus lives in my heart and He goes wherever I go." And I'll never forget what Joe told me. He said, "Well, He ain't going to Baltimore."

— *Bobby Bonner*

For some reason—and to this day I can't explain it—I became a home run hitter. I broke the home run record down in the Class D league at 23 home runs, and they used that Worth ball, which was the deadest ball in baseball. The scouts started looking at me, and finally the Giants' Carl Hubbell came to see me play one night. I hit a home run, and the next day they decided they wanted to buy my contract, so the Giants purchased me for $10,000. They gave that Class D club a couple ballplayers or something.

So in 1950 I started in the Giant chain at Sioux City, Iowa, and I hit 23 home runs there. Back in those days they had a lot of players. I think the Cardinals had 26 farm clubs, so if you're a shortstop you're number 26 on the list trying to get up to the big leagues. All the teams had tons of players. So in '51 I went to spring training with the Triple A club, but they had a guy named Rudy Roofer that was ahead of me, and I just had to take my time and wait and see if he was going do any good, so they sent me to the Cubs' farm club in Nashville on an option. I had an off-season there because I got the mumps. I didn't play half the season. And then in '52 I went to Minneapolis, hit 28 home runs. I think I tied the record in the league for shortstops for home runs, and the Giants called me up at the end of 1952.

— Daryl Spencer

In '64 I started with Richmond, then I went to Rochester, from Rochester to Indianapolis, from Indianapolis to Denver, from Denver to Toronto, and that was the end of it that year. Every time I'd get started—I wasn't playing much—they'd send some young kid in there and they had to play him. I'd be with Rochester, and Darrell Johnson was the manager and he wanted to keep me, but he says, "Rod Sidwell come in, who's about a twenty-two-year-old. I've got to play him, and so I've got to let somebody go. We've got too many shortstops so we've got to let you go." I went to Toronto and finished out the season with Sparky Anderson. I went to spring training with Atlanta, and, of course, I didn't make it. Then I heard Knoxville had an opening for a shortstop. So I went to Knoxville and I said, I'll finish the year, play one more year.

— Don Buddin

The one thing that I enjoyed when I was in the minors, I was sent to El Paso for about three weeks and I was a shortstop, and we had a good little second baseman there, and he and I became very close friends. After the games most of the guys would go out drinking or whatever. We would stay in and get three or four other guys, and we would play the game of *Risk*. We had the best time. Well, that individual was Kurt Russell, and he was making Walt Disney movies back in them days. And then of course he decided to go on and do other movies as well, but he was quite an individual. He was a good little second baseman. He wasn't that big back then, and of course you can't improve your height. He was only like 5'9" I think, and back then he might've been 155 pounds, but you see some of the movies nowadays it makes him look huge and all these muscles, and he's probably put on a little weight here and there. He was a great guy.

— *Bruce Christensen*

The footnote is that San Diego's Triple A team was Hawaii and they did not own that team. They had a working relationship so they provided some players, Hawaii owned some players, and the manager was employed by the Islanders. He was a great guy, Roy Hartsfield. They have a journeyman shortstop, Hector Torres, and Hector's been around a long time, knows what he's doing, and Roy's a veteran manager and he's got to win. So I didn't play much. I was down there for about six weeks, and then I talked to Peter Bavasi

because part of my contract was I was going to be called up in September. Around the first of August I asked him if he could move me to the Double A team, so I could get some playing time in before I got called up, because I really hadn't played since college. I'd only played like once a week. So he did that, which was the Texas League. I was in Alexandria, Louisiana, which was really like a spring training and statistically I didn't do that well, but it worked its purpose. It really got me back in the flow of playing, and then when I went up I felt confident that I was ready.

— *Bill Almon*

The Call Up

I had a real good year in Triple A ball so they bring me up there to spring training. They don't know who the heck I was. There was a guy named Mike Dalehos, really nice guy, a Cuban guy, and they thought he would be the one to go up there. Well, I beat him out at shortstop at Mobile and they put him at second base. I hit .380 something in spring training. I mean, I was hitting the ball really good. Then they're thinking, Who is this guy, you know? So they call me up, and my first nine times at bat I'm 0 for 9. They wouldn't play me. Pinch-hit. Pop up. Pinch-hit. Strikeout. For two months I didn't do nothing but that. Walk, groundout, fly out. I'm 0 for 9. Well, at the end of the season they played me the last ten games, and I hit in like nine games out of 10. I hit about .290 and it made my average like .220. I never really played outside of just going in like that. I was still

mad about it, but that's the way it goes. You were ani-
mals then. I mean, literally. You do what they say or
you're gone. You had really no choice. And, you know,
you're there to play.

— *Jack Kubiszyn*

I'll never forget that day they told me I made the team.
There was no doubt I was supposed to go to Triple A, so
I just had my mind set on that. In fact, I had a car out
there in spring training and they had already sent it to
Denver. [Tom] Trebelhorn's the one that told me. It was
at Phoenix Municipal Stadium. We'd just played the
Oakland A's. I'll never forget it. It was right after the
game. We'd just got through running a few little sprints,
and he called me over and said, "You think you'd like to
go to Milwaukee with us?" I thought, No way. You're kidding. But I said, "Yeah!"

— *Bill Spiers*

Just before I was called up I was in Hawaii playing, and
back then we had seven-game homestands or roadtrips.
I was in Hawaii for seven days, and I had a pretty good
series. I had a couple home runs, a triple, like four doubles, and the rest singles, and I hit like almost .700. It
was unbelievable for seven games, and I was doing a
good job at shortstop. When I was in Hawaii I met a girl,
and her father was a sportswriter for one of the newspa-
pers, and he wanted to do an article on me that first day
that I came in, and we took a bunch of pictures of me
and his daughter, and they had an eight-page layout in

the sports section on me that first game. I was fortunate enough to have a good series. I got back to Salt Lake, and we played that night. My manager was Del Rice in Salt Lake, and he called me up after the game and said, "I've got a call and you're going to The Show." And so I said, "Great." Of course, I was up all night. Flew into LA, my dad picked me up, went to the ballpark at Anaheim there, and Lefty Phillips was the manager, and he says, "Are you ready to play?" And I say, "Yes, I am." So I played that night and went 0 for 4, but at least I played.
— *Bruce Christensen*

I knew I was going, but it's still exciting because the manager of the Double A team was Ken Brace, and Ken was actually the scout who signed me. They had the Double A manager—I think it was Jackie Brandt before I got there—and I think he got sick, and then in a real quick move they just sent Ken down there for the last six weeks of the season to run the team. He just gave me a rundown of what I was to look for and stuff like that. Which was very helpful, but it was still extremely exciting.
— *Bill Almon*

It was pretty cool. It was kind of a culmination of everything you've been working for. But at the same time, if I remember right, we were at Triple A, and we had played the whole year, and we were just entering the playoffs. I think the playoffs were a couple days away for our Triple A team, so you're thinking, Oh man, I'm not going to be here with the guys for that. But that lasts about two

seconds and then you think, Where's the team? Where am I joining the team?
— *Paul Zuvella*

3ᴿᴰ

A Shortstop's Timeline

1869

Transcendental Graphics

August 30
1900

"Bad Bill" Dahlen, who currently stands fifth in the National League for career games played at shortstop, hits 2 triples in the eighth inning of a game against Philadelphia to lead the Brooklyn Superbas to a 14-3 victory.

Former cricket player **George Wright** is the shortstop for the Cincinnati Red Stockings, baseball's first openly all professional team. Wright hits a remarkable 47 home runs in just 59 games and compiles a batting average of .633. He is inducted into the Baseball Hall of Fame as an Executive/Pioneer in 1937.

July 19
1909

Shortstop **Neal Ball** of the Cleveland Naps
completes the first unassisted triple play in
major league history against the Boston Red
Sox when he catches a line drive off the bat
of Amby McConnell, steps on second to double off Heinie Wagner, and tags Jake Stahl
coming off first. That same day Ball will hit
the first home run of his career.

October 1
1903

The first World Series game is
played with the Boston Americans
facing the Pittsburgh Pirates.
Honus Wagner starts at short for
the Pirates while Freddy Parent
gets the nod for the hometown
Americans. In all likelihood the
greatest shortstop of all-time, Wagner leads the league in hitting
eight times, in RBI and stolen
bases five times each, and becomes
one of the five original Hall of
Fame inductees.

53

Transcendental Graphics

June 20
1914

Shortstop **Ray Chapman** of the Cleveland Naps sets a major league record by committing four errors in the fifth inning of a 7-1 loss to the New York Yankees. Six years later an inside fastball thrown by Yankee submarine pitcher Carl Mays will hit Chapman in the head and he will die the following day. This is the first incident of a pitched ball resulting in death in baseball history.

May 18
1912

When Ty Cobb's Tiger teammates refuse to play in protest of the center fielder's suspension, Detroit owner Frank Navin instructs his manager, Hughie Jennings, to suit up local amateurs to avoid a threatened $5,000 league fine. Thus, shortstop **Vincent Maney** plays his only major league game. Maney goes 0 for 2 with a walk and commits one error as the Philadelphia Athletics beat the replacement Tigers 24-2.

May 1
1924

Chicago White Sox shortstop **"Whispering Bill" Barrett** steals home twice, once in the first inning and once in the ninth, in a game against Cleveland. The White Sox win 13-7 as Barrett ties a major league record. However, his .904 fielding percentage for the year is the league's worst and though his major league career will last another six seasons he will play but four more games at shortstop.

July 6
1933

1925

The Washington Senators' **Roger Peckinpaugh**, despite leading the American League in exactly zero statistical categories, becomes the first shortstop in either league to be named MVP. Unfortunately, in the World Series Peckinpaugh commits a Series record eight errors, including two in the seventh and deciding game to allow the Pittsburgh Pirates to defeat the Senators four games to three. The following year Peckinpaugh loses his starting role to Buddy Myer and in 1927 is traded to the White Sox for his final, abbreviated season.

The first All-Star game is played at Chicago's Comiskey Park. **Dick "Rowdy Richard" Bartell** starts at short for the National League while future Hall of Famer **Joe Cronin** starts for the American League. A two-run, third-inning homer by Babe Ruth off pitcher Bill Hallahan gives the Americans a lead they won't relinquish as they win 4-2.

55

The SHORTSTOP

April 29
1934

Luis Aparicio is born in Mara-
caibo, Venezuela. Aparicio will
win the American League Rookie of the Year in 1956, lead the
league in stolen bases 10 times,
be selected for 10 All-Star
games, win 9 Gold Glove
Awards and play more games at
short than any other player in
major league history before his
Hall of Fame induction in 1984.

1944

Marty Marion of the St. Loui
Cardinals becomes the firs
shortstop to win the Nationa
League MVP. Though Mario
will bat just .227 in the post
season, the Cardinals will bes
their crosstown rival St. Loui
Browns four games to two t
capture their second Worl
Series title in three years

Transcendental Graphics

1950 After finishing second in MVP voting the prior season, the New York Yankees' **Phil "Scooter" Rizzuto** is named American League MVP. In the post-season the Yanks will sweep Philadelphia's Whiz Kids to become the fourth of seven World's Champions Rizzuto will play for. Rizzuto will be inducted into the Hall of Fame in 1994.

1948

Player/manager **Lou Boudreau** of the Cleveland Indians bats a career high .355 and becomes the second shortstop to be named American League MVP. The Indians will go on to defeat the Boston Braves in the World Series four games to two, Boudreau's only World's Championship as either player or manager. In 1970 Boudreau will be inducted into the Hall of Fame.

Transcendental Graphics

1957

Roy McMillan of the Cincinnati Reds becomes the first Rawlings Gold Glove shortstop. It is the first of three consecutive Gold Gloves McMillan wins in a career that includes more than 2,000 games at the position.

Transcendental Graphics

1958

"Mr. Cub" Ernie Banks hits 47 home runs to lead the National League and collects the first of two consecutive MVP awards. In 1960 Banks will win the Gold Glove for shortstops but play his last game as a middle infielder just one year later. In his 19-year career Banks will actually play 134 more games at first than at short.

October 13
1960

In Game 7 of the 1960 World Series, the Pittsburgh Pirates trail the Yankees 7-4 in the eighth inning when, with Gino Cimoli on first, outfielder Bill Virdon hit a routine ground ball to New York shortstop **Tony Kubek**. The ball, however, takes a nasty hop and strikes Kubek in the throat. Virdon's grounder is ruled a base hit and leads to a five-run Pirate eighth. Kubek is taken to a hospital for overnight treatment. And while the Yankees come back to tie the game in the top of the ninth, Bill Mazeroski's leadoff home run off Ralph Terry in the bottom of the inning will bring the Pirates their first World's Championship in 35 years.

1960

Dick Groat of the Pittsburgh Pirates leads the National League with a .325 batting average and becomes the third shortstop in as many years to be named MVP.

August 3
1962

Batting eighth, Cleveland Indians shortstop **Jack Kubiszyn** hits his first and only major league home run off Kansas City's Bill Fischer to propel the Tribe to a 1-0 victory. It marks the thirteenth time a first home run will win a 1-0 ballgame in the majors and the first time it's been done by a shortstop.

July 23
1964

In the first inning of a game against the Minnesota Twins, Kansas City Athletics shortstop **Bert Campaneris** homers against Jim Kaat in his first major league at-bat. Campaneris takes Kaat deep again in the seventh inning and the A's win 4-3 in eleven innings. Campaneris will hit just 77 more home runs in his 19-year career.

July 9
1971

Atlanta Braves shortstop **Leo Foster** makes his major league debut by committing an error on the first ball hit to him, hitting into a double play in his first at-bat and then hitting into the first triple play recorded at Three Rivers Stadium as the Pirates stomp the Braves 11-2.

1965

Shortstop **Zoilo Versalles** of the Minnesota Twins becomes the first foreign-born player to win an MVP award. Despite striking out a career- and league-high 122 times and managing a mere .273 batting average, Versalles leads the American League in at-bats, runs, doubles, triples, total bases, and extra-base hits. In the post-season, the Twins will lose to the Los Angeles Dodgers in the first World Series to be played in Minnesota.

April 26
1974

Pittsburgh shortstop **Mario Mendoza**, who will inspire the term "Mendoza Line," makes his major league debut against the Astros when he pinch runs for Pirates slugger Willie Stargell after Stargell is hit in the head by a pitch to lead off the bottom half of the ninth. Mendoza later scores to tie the game and a subsequent error by Houston shortstop **Roger Metzger** brings home the winning run. Though the Mendoza Line signifies a batting average of .200, Mendoza, who also played for Seattle and Texas over nine major league seasons, actually finished with a career mark of .215.

October 8
1973

In the fifth inning of Game Three of the National League Championship Series, Pete Rose, whose Cincinnati Reds trail the hometown Mets 9-2, triggers a bench-clearing brawl by taking out New York shortstop **Bud Harrelson** at second base. Though the double play was completed and little damage occurred during the standoff (save for a Mets hat that is torn apart by Reds reliever Pedro Bordon's teeth), the game is halted in the bottom half of the inning as Shea Stadium fans shower Rose with debris. The remainder of the game is played with New York City police surrounding the field. The Mets go on to take the pennant three games to two.

August 10 Orioles shortstop **Cal Ripken Jr.** enters his first major league
1981 game as a pinch-runner for Ken Singleton in the twelfth
inning of a game against the Kansas City Royals. The debut is
a success as John Lowenstein later singles Ripken home with
the winning run.

May 30 Batting eighth, and playing
1982 third base, **Cal Ripken Jr.** begins
his streak of 2,632 consecutive
games. The streak continues
until September 20, 1998, the
Orioles' final home game of the
season.

1982

After a 17-year
drought, Milwaukee
Brewer **Robin Yount**
will claim the MVP
Award for American
League shortstops.
Yount will be select-
ed as MVP once
again in 1989, but
as an outfielder. An
All-Star selection a
mere three times in
his career, Yount
will enter the Hall
of Fame in 1999.

Rich Pilling/Major League Baseball/Getty Images

October 13
1984

One-half of the most recognizable double-play combination since Joe Tinker and Johnny Evers, Detroit shortstop **Alan Trammell** reaches the pinnacle of his playing career by belting a pair of 2-run homers, each time driving in his partner Lou Whitaker, accounting for all four Tiger runs in Game Four of the World Series. The Tigers will close out a four games to one Series victory over the Padres the following night, and Trammell is named Series MVP.

1990

Cal Ripken Jr. sets a major league record by committing just three errors at shortstop over the course of the season. White Sox shortstop **Ozzie Guillen** commits 17 errors and wins the American League Gold Glove. Ripken will claim the first of his two Gold Glove Awards the following season.

Ezra Shaw / Getty Images Sport / Getty Images

July 9
1991

After winning the Home
Run Derby contest the day
before, **Cal Ripken Jr.'s**
3-run roundtripper leads the
American League to a 4-2
win, its fourth consecutive
All-Star victory, and Ripken
is named the game's MVP.

July 15
1993

In Baltimore, **Cal Ripken Jr.**
hits his 278th homer, a three-
run shot off Scott Erickson to
pass **Ernie Banks** for the most
by a shortstop. The Orioles
beat the Twins 5-3.

July 8
1994

After being selected the number one overall pick in the baseball draft just one year before, Seattle Mariners shortstop **Alex Rodriguez** makes his major league debut. He is the youngest player to start a major league game in 16 years.

1995   Cincinnati Reds shortstop **Barry Larkin** steals a career-high 51 bases, wins his second of three consecutive Gold Glove Awards, and becomes the first National League shortstop to claim the MVP Award in 35 seasons.

Matthew Stockman/Getty Images Sport/Getty Images

July 9
1996

Five years to the day after being selected All-Star Game MVP, **Cal Ripken Jr.** returns to the Summer Classic only to suffer one of the most serious injuries of his career when White Sox pitcher Roberto Hernandez slips during the team photo shoot and breaks Ripken's nose with his forearm. Ripken starts the game nonetheless.

1999

Red Sox shortstop **Nomar Garciaparra** blasts three home runs, including two grand slams, in a 12-4 Boston win over the Mariners. Garciaparra hits his first slam off Seattle starter Brett Hinchcliffe in the first inning, takes Hinchcliffe deep again with one man on in the third, and finishes with a grand slam in the eighth against reliever Eric Weaver for a one-day total of 10 RBI. It marks the only time a shortstop has hit two grand slams in a single game.

October 4
1999

On the last day of the regular season, Mets shortstop **Rey Ordonez** completes his 100th consecutive game without an error to sets a major league record in a 5-0 victory over the Reds. At season's end he collects his third consecutive Gold Glove Award. The celebration lasts all of one off-season and one game as Ordonez commits an error in the first inning of the second game of 2000.

2000

Rafael Furcal is the first shortstop to win the National League Rookie of the Year award. Though **Alvin Dark**, as a member of the National League Boston Braves, was named Rookie of the Year in 1948, only one award, covering both leagues, was given. In the interim, eleven American League shortstops have been named.

Alex Rodriguez of the Texas Rangers, the highest-paid player in baseball, leads the American League in slugging percentage, runs, home runs and collects his second consecutive Gold Glove Award on the way to being selected American League MVP. The pick, however, is somewhat controversial in that the Rangers finished last in the league's Western Division, a full twenty games below .500. The following season Rodriguez will debut in a new uniform (the Yankees) at a new position (third base), marking the first time a defending MVP has been traded, as well as the first time a defending Gold Glove winner changed positions.

2003

2005

Omar Vizquel of the San Francisco Giants wins his 10th Gold Glove Award. The Giants are the third team for which he has won the award. In 1993, he won his first with the Seattle Mariners, followed by eight more between 1994 and 2001 with the Cleveland Indians.

MLB

67

4TH

A Day in the Life—Jose Valentin

Jose Valentin is open, patient, forthright. But he does not want to discuss what time he wakes on Tuesday, August 26, 2003.

"Whatever I feel like," he says.

Sure. Of course. The man's making $5 million to play shortstop for the Chicago White Sox this season, and he doesn't have to be at work until, well, not until mid-afternoon anyway.

So what time did he get up this morning?

"Probably tomorrow," Valentin responds. "Because my wife is here."

Okay. I'm from Alabama. I have an accent. Jose Valentin's from Puerto Rico. He has an accent. But for twenty minutes we've been able to understand each other just fine.

"But what about today?" I ask.

"Probably tomorrow," Valentin says, "it'll be earlier than today because she's leaving tomorrow early in the morning."

"So you slept late today is what you're saying."

"Exactly," he says.

So whatever time Jose Valentin crawls out of bed in his hotel next to New York's Grand Central Terminal, it's later than he wants to admit. But when he does get up, he goes shopping with his wife, Ilka.

"Pretty much," Valentin says. "That's the only reason why she came here."

Valentin even takes a commercial flight from Chicago to New York following Sunday's home game against the Rangers. The rest of the White Sox come in on Monday's team charter. And so Valentin is doing the good husband thing, going around with his wife on the New York City shopping trip.

"I was trying, yeah."

So on this morning when Jose Valentin sleeps late and shops with his wife, he arrives at Yankee Stadium, on the White Sox team bus, at 4:20 in the afternoon. And like nearly every major leaguer to ever enter a visitor's clubhouse, Jose Valentin places a bag down by his locker and walks to the ticket table in the middle of the room to arrange his pass list for this evening's game. It will be the 1,263rd contest of his major league career. And though he's shown some versatility in the field, both at the amateur and professional levels, all but 195 of those games have been at shortstop.

And yet Jose Valentin is not your typical shortstop. For starters, his defense, as might be surmised by his compulsory adaptations, has, at times, been suspect. Though he is an undisputed leader on the infield and can, on occasion, deliver highlight-quality plays, he

Karan Rinaldo

JOSE VALENTIN

committed a major-league-high 37 errors in 1996, his first year with more than 120 games at the position. Only the Rockies' Walt Weiss made as many as 30 errors that season.

Valentin's return to the American League, when he joined the White Sox in 2000, also saw another escalation in his error count: 36 that season. In contrast, only one other major league shortstop, Desi Relaford, who divided his time between Philadelphia and San Diego, committed as many as 30. American League Gold Glove winner Omar Vizquel made but three errors, Kansas City shortstop Rey Sanchez committed just four, and Mark Loretta, the shortstop who replaced Valentin in Milwaukee, committed just two in 2000, albeit in an abbreviated 90 appearances.

Jose Valentin is also an awkward fit for the offensive shortstop mold. His listed size (5'10" 185 pounds) is that of a shortstop, but the man has deceptive power.

"That was my numbers early in my career. When I was 21," Valentin says. "Now I'm 33. I put some weight on a little bit. I probably go 195 right now. And I think 5'10" is wrong. I'm a little smaller than that. But a lot of people say, Well, this guy is kind of a small guy. There's no way this guy can hit the ball far. But I get a lot of people by surprise the way I hit the ball. I just go up there and try to hit the ball hard."

Since being traded from the Brewers in January of 2000, Valentin has hit at least 25 home runs in each of his three full White Sox seasons. Entering today's game against the Yankees he's already hit 21. After two years, 1998 and 1999, of hitting less than .230 for the Brewers, Valentin's average also improved once he arrived in Chicago. But while his power numbers have remained steady, his batting average, since that initial "welcome to the Windy City" rise, has fallen: .273 in 2000, .258 in 2001, .249 in 2002. Today Valentin's average stands at .238.

Most distressing for the switch-hitter, or at the very least his manager Jerry Manuel, is the difference between his batting average against left-handed and right-handed pitching. In 2000, his best year as a hitter, Valentin played in 141 games at short. He hit .282 vs. right-handers but just .215 against lefties. 24 of his 25 home runs came against right-handed pitching. In 2001, he split his time—66 games at third, 43 games at short, and 24 games in center field. He hit .263 against right-handers and .203 against lefties. All but three of his 28 home runs came against right-handed pitching.

In 2002, Valentin, at the club's request, tried his hand as the everyday third baseman. He finished the year with 83 games at third and 50 at short. He hit .259 against right-handers and a woeful .152 against lefties. Of his 25 home runs, only one came against right-handed pitching.

In 2003, Joe Crede arrived from the White Sox farm system to take over third base. Valentin returned to shortstop, and by season's end his batting average against right-handed pitching more than doubled his average against left-handers. Though he's been a switch-hitter throughout his twelve-year major league career, he admits to giving at least brief thought to becoming strictly a left-handed hitter.

"I'm really a lefty naturally," he says, "but I cannot make my right side the same way as the left side. It's just like I cannot be the same hitter."

But just because thought has been given does not mean a change is imminent.

"It's something that at this level," Valentin says, "you can't go out there and try."

The last time he did try, the last time he faced a left-handed pitcher while batting from the left side of the plate, was four years earlier, in this very stadium. The experiment did not go well. The at-bat remains in his mind.

"It was here against [Mike] Stanton," Valentin says, "and I got three pitches, three breaking balls, and it was a joke. Like I said, this is not a level to go there and try. If you play in the big leagues, you have to get it done. And to try to go hit on one side, go back to the minor leagues, that doesn't work. I came up here, in the big leagues, as a switch-hitter, and now that I've got ten years in the big leagues, why?"

But things in August of 2003 are looking up, both for Jose Valentin and the Chicago White Sox. After a disastrous mid-August road trip to Anaheim and Texas nearly cost the Sox any lingering hope to reach this year's playoffs, the team turned the tables when the Angels and Rangers visited Comiskey. Coming into tonight's game in New York, the Sox have won six of their last seven games to move to seven games over .500. This is not shocking. For the 2003 season Chicago will finish 21 games above .500 at home, and 11 games below .500 on the road.

Jose Valentin's homestand was personally successful as well. The shortstop went 6 for 21 with three home runs and committed just one error. Plus, he received more playing time with Roberto Alomar, his middle infield partner of less than two months. On July 1 the

New York Mets washed their hands of the twelve-time All-Star and ten-time Gold Glove second baseman when they sent him, and cash, for two little-used relief pitchers and a career minor leaguer.

Alomar's locker with his new team is on the veteran's wall, all the way left, farthest from the clubhouse entrance and closest to the off-limits-to-the-press training room. Valentin's locker is to his right, and to Valentin's right is Sox slugger Magglio Ordonez. Both Valentin and Ordonez will talk to the press before tonight's game. Alomar will not. And when his name is announced in the starting lineup, Alomar will be heartily booed by New York fans. It is his first trip back to the city since the trade.

But even if New Yorkers aren't happy to see Alomar, Valentin is certainly excited to have the future Hall of Famer on his team.

"He's one of the best in the game," Valentin says. "When you have a guy like that you feel comfortable at shortstop. No matter what kind of throw you make. A lot of second basemen say, When you're going to toss me the ball, just toss me a little bit to my left so I can get more motion. They only feel comfortable in one place. With Alomar it's different. Alomar says, Just go ahead and throw me the ball and I'll do the rest. He knows how to make adjustments to try to help you out."

At 5:15 Jose Valentin exits the visitor's clubhouse and walks through the tunnel to the visitor's dugout at Yankee Stadium. By 5:17 he is exchanging warm-up tosses with Alomar. The Yankees have the field for batting practice until 5:40, so after loosening a bit Valentin is interviewed by a Spanish language radio station.

Valentin and Alomar are in the White Sox second batting practice group. Coach Art Kusnyer, a right-handed thrower (tonight's starter for the Yankees, Roger Clemens, is, of course, a right-hander) and the man who caught Nolan Ryan's second major league no-hitter, does the pitching honors.

In the batting cage, Valentin pulls everything. This is not hyperbole. The man literally pulls every pitch. Kusnyer's second offering to Valentin ends up in the right field bleachers. Several more balls follow its path.

"I'm a natural pull hitter," Valentin explains. "That's my strength. You don't want to go all BP just to try to go opposite way. Especially tonight. You're not going to be able to try to go opposite way with a guy like Clemens. That's a power pitcher there so you want to use your hands. You might see some balls go the opposite way. I might sometime try to look for something that way and try to go there, but you won't see that too often from me."

With each cage session Valentin takes a few swings from the right side to finish his turn. He hits the first pitch weakly to short. The second pitch goes farther, but would've been an easy fly to left. In his next rotation he takes a few swings with an aluminum bat.

"A lot of guys think [you should] just use your hands," he says. "It's kind of light and pretty much you know the ball's going to jump better than using the wood bat so what you have to do is not swing too hard. Just use your hands."

Following batting practice Valentin and his teammates return to the locker room. White Sox infielders, both starters and bench players, meet with tonight's starting pitcher, Esteban Loiaza, tonight's starting catcher, Miguel Olivo, and first base coach and former shortstop Rafael Santana who assists with defensive positioning.

"We go through how we're going to play each individual hitter," Valentin says. The pitcher's preference as to how he wants to pitch a certain batter, of course, reigns. But Valentin makes it clear that the infielders, especially those veterans like himself and Alomar, have input. "If he says, We're going to play Jeter to pull," Valentin says, "then I'll say, Wait, Jeter likes to hit the ball inside out. Or it depends on the count, so we're going to play pull early in the count, or late in the count we're going to move towards you or whatever. Those are the comments that we make."

Valentin's responsibilities as shortstop do not end there. Compared to third base, Valentin's primary position in 2002, well, there's really no comparison.

"At shortstop," he says, "even if you don't get the ball you always have to be ready for anything. The communication with the pitchers. Pop-ups. Any pop-outs to left field, you always have to go get them, go get the relay, or the ground ball to second base. Force out at second. Or ground ball to the pitcher, double play, or groundball to first base. You always have to want to get a double play with the first baseman. At third base, you don't get too many balls. The only thing, when you get one, it's coming hot, because that's the only way. But at third base you only have to go one side, which is the right side. At shortstop you have to be ready right, left, back, forward. You always have to be in the game."

Valentin also keeps an eye on the catcher's signals to help, not only with his positioning, but the positioning of the entire infield.

"The way I move," he says, "sometimes it depends on the hitter. It depends on the count. I like to know what signs my pitcher's using, so that way I can kind of cheat to be ready. You can make your first move or react down there."

The signs, of course, change with runners on base.

"With men on second," Valentin says, "you use different signs. When there's a guy on first we only go first sign."

Valentin is also responsible for relaying certain pitches to Joe Crede at third.

"If it's a breaking ball against a righty, I just call his name—Joe or Crede or Be ready—but only on breaking balls. And not too early either, because if you call it early then the hitter will be able to hear it or something. You have to be careful how you give the sign to him because you don't want him to move early and then the hitter pick him up and know the location."

When there's a potential base stealer on first, there are the signs to Alomar—open mouth or closed mouth, hidden behind Valentin's glove—to establish which one of them will take the catcher's throw to second.

"Open is he got him, closed I got him," Valentin says. "It depends on who's the hitter. If it's a left-hander, most of the time I'm going to cover second. If it's a righthander hitter, if it's a guy that likes to hit and run, hit the ball the other way, then I might just switch the signs. It depends on the pitcher. It depends on the situation and the count."

Of course, there's also the more lucrative offensive side to the position. In the good old days, say the '60s and '70s, it was enough that a shortstop be steady defensively. Not anymore. Today the position comes with a certain amount of offensive expectation. And tonight Valentin will be facing Roger Clemens.

"Clemens is a guy that throws a lot of cutters, a split-finger," Valentin says. "That's pretty much his pitches. He's not going to throw me a lot of breaking balls. He's a power guy so you're going to see some fastballs, and when you get two strikes, pretty much you're going to see the split finger, so make sure that you get your fast-ball early in the count."

Tonight Clemens' mother, Bess, who suffers from emphysema and missed her son's 300th victory is on hand to throw the ceremonial first pitch. She rides a golf cart to the first base line and, with her son's assistance, half-tosses the ball to the waiting catcher. Clemens hugs his mother, who cries at the embrace, and then makes his way to the mound. This will be Clemens' 600th career start. It will also be one of his worst.

After the game Clemens is asked about his mother's appearance.

"It was great," he said. "They should have let her stay on the mound. She had better stuff than I had."

But the top of the first goes smoothly for him. Alomar flies out to left, Carlos Lee grounds out to third, and Frank Thomas is caught looking at an outside fastball. Valentin jogs onto the field, to the edge of the outfield grass. Paul Konerko, the first baseman, tosses a grounder that crawls up Valentin's left arm. Call it an E6 on the warm-up. When he retrieves the ball he tosses a bouncer back to the first baseman. Valentin aligns himself between second and third, in effect creating a triangle with himself as the movable top point.

"I just look from third base towards second base," he says, "and you see that angle. Because not every infield in baseball is the same. From the edge, from the infield grass to all the way back, they're not the same. Like here's a lot smaller than our place, the way this angle is in Yankee Stadium. Because it's a lot different, you might not feel the same way the first day. It's probably going to take a couple of innings to get used to it, because this is the first time that we play in Yankee Stadium this year."

But Valentin adjusts quickly enough. He plays a step inside the outfield grass and the night's first ball put in play, hit by Yankees second baseman Alfonso Soriano, comes right to him. Valentin comes in a step to meet the ball and throws to first for the out.

"Actually it was the first and the only one I got all

game," he says of Soriano's grounder. "I don't think we had too many groundballs. I think there were about four or five. It was something to get you in the game right away. If you make the first one, you're like, Okay, I made the first one so I'm ready to make the other one. If you miss the first one, it's like, Well, I got the bad one right away, so just get ready for the next one. But you don't want to just wait for the situation when it's close in the game and then you haven't been able to get a ground ball and then you have one and boot it."

The White Sox infield shifts slightly left for the left-handed batting Nick Johnson who strikes out against Loiaza. Then Derek Jeter grounds weakly to the pitcher for the final out of the inning.

Magglio Ordonez leads off the White Sox second by missing a high Clemens fastball, and Carl Everett waves at an outside fastball for Clemens' third strikeout of the game. The White Sox first baseman, Paul Konerko, moves into the batter's box and Valentin enters the on-deck circle. The shortstop puts white batting gloves on both hands, and briefly maintains the appearance of a butler about to serve tea. He holds his bat on his left shoulder. Only occasionally does he put the bat in motion, a roundabout counter-clockwise movement, but this is just nervous energy while Konerko deposits Clemens' 2-2 pitch in the screen just past the left centerfield fence and the White Sox lead 1-0.

Valentin touches hands with Konerko after he crosses home and steps in to bat left-handed against the Yan-

Karan Rinaldo

JOSE VALENTIN

kee pitcher. For this at-bat at least, Valentin adopts a somewhat closed stance, planting his back foot, his left foot in this instance, first. Valentin says that his stance is not too dissimilar from that of Yankees' designated hitter Jason Giambi.

"But I'm not always like that," he says. "It just depends who's the pitcher, who's facing me. You have to make adjustments every at-bat because you might face a guy three times in one game, so you've got to make your adjustment to the way he pitches. If they pitch me inside all game, then I just go to the wide open stance, to be able to get myself more freedom to be able to get that pitch inside and turn on it."

There's little doubt that Jose Valentin is an attacking hitter. He likes the first pitch. Hell, he loves the first pitch. Valentin, in fact, is batting over .300 when he puts the first pitch in play.

"I like to be aggressive," Valentin says. "I don't take too many pitches. That's my plan for Clemens. Be aggressive. I'm looking fastball. I probably won't see a fastball all the time, but that's what I'm looking for."

Of course, Roger Clemens knows this. His first pitch is a breaking ball away, but this time at least that's what Valentin is looking for. His timing's right, but his swing is just under. The ball is fouled straight back into the upper deck.

"I've faced him a lot of times," Valentin says of Clemens, "and he's pretty much working away to me. Throws a lot of backdoor pitches, breaking ball away, cutters away, and the split-finger. I will sit looking for something away, but he's a guy who won't give in. He will not give you something to hit, so you've got to go up there and be aggressive because he's tough. You cannot take pitches and get in a hole. You've got to be aggressive, try to get a good pitch the first couple of pitches, and make sure that when you get it, don't miss it."

That first pitch, Valentin recalls, would be the best one Clemens would throw him all night.

"The rest was all kind of tough," he says. "Like I say, he might give you one pitch to hit and you better swing and make contact with it because you're not going to see too many good pitches off him."

Clemens's second pitch stays high. The third is a breaking ball low and away. Valentin fouls it off and grimaces, not from pain but rather frustration.

"Right when he let it go you could see it was a ball," he says. "It was something that I was pretty much guessing. I would go there and swing no matter what was the pitch, and I was pretty much out of my plan."

With Clemens ahead in the count a ball and two strikes, Valentin lifts an outside pitch high into left centerfield where it is caught by Bernie Williams for the third out.

"That was another split-finger," he says, "but it just kind of hung. I was pretty much protecting myself to not strike out."

Giambi leads off the bottom of the second for the Yankees, and Valentin is positioned like a second baseman against a right-handed pull hitter, on the first-base side of second, on the lip of the outfield grass. The positioning pays off. Giambi pops up high above Valentin's head. The shortstop calls for it, takes a couple of steps without really moving, and catches the ball for the first out. Bernie Williams walks, the Yankees' first baserunner, and Valentin, back at his normal shortstop position now that Giambi has been retired, plays a step farther in from the outfield, a step closer to the bag.

The Yankees catcher, Jorge Posada, fouls out to third baseman Joe Crede, who runs in almost to home plate to corral the pop up. Valentin comes in to talk to pitcher Loiaza behind the mound, and then jogs back to position. For lefty Karim Garcia, Valentin shades another step toward second and a step farther back toward the outfield grass. But Garcia is jammed on the pitch, knocking a broken bat loop to short left center. Valentin points up as he runs into the outfield, then points to second to direct Carlos Lee's throw, coming in behind Bernie Williams who trips as he rounds second base.

"I could see him running and looking at the ball and not looking at the base," Valentin says, "and that's why he tripped on top of the base and fell. I was trying to tell Carlos to go to second, but I guess he didn't throw the ball right away."

Even if Lee had returned the ball quickly, Williams would've managed to get back safely as his fall left him within arm's reach of the bag. Valentin walks over to check on him.

"I asked him if he was okay," he says. "It looked pretty bad, and it's the guy that already got knee surgery so you don't know what happened. I could tell he was hurt. I guess he was kind of embarrassed. He was kind of laughing."

With runners on first and second and two out,

Valentin does his best to hold Williams close to the base, well aware that he'll likely score on a base hit.

"I'm just making noise," Valentin says. "I'm trying to be obvious. I try to be obvious to let him know, Hey Bernie, I'm here. I won't say nothing like that but I will make some noises to let him know that I'm close to him."

Leftfielder David Dellucci works Loiaza to a 3-2 count, then fouls off the payoff pitch. With another one coming, Valentin stands directly behind Williams until Loiaza goes into his motion to deliver strike three.

Third baseman Joe Crede leads off the third inning by crushing a 2-0 fastball to give the White Sox a 2-0 lead. In the bottom half of the inning, Yankee third baseman Enrique Wilson grounds to first to bring up the top of the order. As they did the first time, Valentin shades second baseman Alfonso Soriano toward third while Crede creeps in to the third base cutout. With two strikes, Crede steps back and Soriano goes down swinging. Valentin turns to his outfielders with two fingers held high. When first baseman Nick Johnson works Loiaza to a 3-1 count, Valentin backs up a step. Johnson walks.

With Derek Jeter at the plate Valentin again steps toward third. With the count 0-1 Valentin comes in a step. Jeter swings and misses for strike two and catcher Olivo fires down to first to try and pick off Johnson. The play is close but Johnson is safe. It doesn't matter. Jeter goes down swinging for strike three.

In the top of the fourth Frank Thomas leads off by striking out swinging on an inside fastball, his second strikeout in two at-bats. Magglio Ordonez takes a 3-2 pitch
low and inside to walk before Carl Everett, also for the
second time in two at-bats, strikes out swinging against
Clemens.

Valentin returns to the on-deck circle. He takes two
full left-handed cuts, then tight, abbreviated swings, as if
he's using the weight of the bat and its sudden motion
to crack his wrists. As he rests with the bat on his left
shoulder, Paul Konerko doubles against the right-cen-
terfield wall scoring Ordonez. Konerko tries for the
third on the throw home, but the throw beats him, badly, and Konerko appears to be waiting for the inevitable.
But there's no one at second base. Third base coach
Bruce Kimm waves for Konerko to go back, but the first
baseman, once again, is late. He's out at second in a
scorekeeper's special, 9 to 4 to 2 to 5 to 6, but the White
Sox lead 3-0.

Jason Giambi leads off the fourth inning as he did in the
second. Again, Valentin swings around to the first base
side of second. He's not even a full step in front of the
outfield grass when the DH lines out to center. It's back
to his regular position for Bernie Williams, a switch-hitter, who skies the first pitch to Carlos Lee in left. Posada
grounds to first to end the Yankee half of the fourth.

Valentin leads off the Chicago fifth. While Clemens
takes his warm-ups the shortstop leans against the blue
padded posts in front of the White Sox dugout while

putting on his batting gloves. He glances up at the press box, takes a roundhouse, counter-clockwise swing followed by a short, quarter-length swing, and steps into the batter's box.

He stands up on the plate, takes a fastball outside for ball one. He fouls the second pitch back, and with Posada set up outside, skies Clemens' third offering to his counterpart Jeter at short. Valentin begins to remove his batting gloves before reaching the dugout. It is right about now, as Jose Valentin walks down the three steps to the White Sox bench, that Roger Clemens' night falls apart.

Joe Crede singles to left. Catcher Miguel Olivo triples over Bernie Williams' head in center to score Crede. The Yankees, now down 4-0, bring the infield in for Alomar who walks. Clemens starts Carlos Lee with a ball, and pitching coach Mel Stottlemyre, despite having no one up in the bullpen, comes out to talk. Lee works a full count, then takes the payoff pitch low. The bases are loaded for Frank Thomas who has struck out twice in two at-bats. Not this time. Thomas hits a grand slam, a towering drive off the left field foul pole at upper deck height. It is the eighth grand slam of his career and, in a bit of kismet, the White Sox now lead 8-0.

"What went through my mind was like it was a big blowout," Valentin says of Thomas' home run. "That punch right there was a knockout. The way Loiaza was pitching, they looked like they were real uncomfortable at home plate, like they had no chance, so as soon as Frank hit that home run, I said, Well, this is it. We got 'em."

To add insult to injury, Magglio Ordonez, on a 1-0 offering, hits his second home run of the night into the black seats in right center. The White Sox now lead 9-0.

When Carl Everett comes to the plate, the crowd is buzzing. Clemens has allowed four home runs in a game for the just the second time in his major league career. In the bullpen, Chris Hammond, who rose to warm up following the Thomas home run, begins to throw harder. Everett grounds out to second for the second out of the inning.

Paul Konerko, already 2 for 2 against Clemens this evening, comes to bat. Valentin steps to the on-deck circle, but now he carries a natural wood bat and parks it on his right shoulder. In his two prior trips the bat was black and rested on his left.

The black bat that he used against Clemens is a Carolina Club. The natural, or blonde bat, is an Old Hickory brand. All of Valentin's bats are 34 inches in length, but some weigh 31 ounces and some weigh 33 ½.

"I've got some Old Hickory, I've got Carolina Clubs. I've got some Louisville Sluggers. I've got all kinds of bats," Valentin says.

He enters the on-deck circle with the lighter bat because he's certain that no matter how Konerko fares, he will not face Clemens again.

"I already faced Clemens twice," he says. "The gate [bullpen] was open already. The way he was getting hit, there's just no way I get my chances off him. They're not going to let him give up another three-run homer and put the score 11-0."

Konerko walks, and sure enough, in comes Chris Hammond, a lefty, from the bullpen.

"I faced him when he was in Atlanta," Valentin says. "He's a guy that's pretty much just off-speed. Good changeup."

Valentin takes a ball inside, then another outside. He gets under the 2-0 pitch and flies out to Bernie Williams in center.

"I'm not used to seeing a lot of lefties," he says. "And when you don't see too many lefties, every time they bring you one that's the weaker side so you just kind of feel uncomfortable. And that was the problem yesterday. Even though I faced him before, I've been facing a righty the whole game, a guy throwing 94, 95, and then a left-handed pitcher who only throws 85. I mean, you're going to feel uncomfortable.

"It's easier if you face a guy in the beginning with less velocity, than to go hard to soft, because you've already been through the situation where your bat had to speed up to face a guy like Clemens. You already got two at-bats where you try to be quicker, and then you face a guy that throws 85 with a lot of change-ups. So then to stay back is tough. Even though you know the guy doesn't throw hard, it's hard to make adjustments sometimes."

Of course, a 9-0 score instills a certain dynamic into the at-bat as well.

"I'm not going to hit too many home runs from the right side," he says, "so I don't think the guy's going to throw a breaking ball or changeup when the game's already out of reach. Especially when he knows I'm not a dangerous hitter on the right side. So I thought he might try the fastball right away, try to get ahead. And if I took it for a strike I probably wouldn't see anymore fastballs. Then changeup, slider. So I just tried to get a fastball to hit, but that pitch was kind of low and in, and I took it for a ball."

Hammond's second pitch was also a ball, yet the selection surprised Valentin.

"It was a changeup," he says. "Even though the first pitch was a ball, he threw me a changeup."

So with the count 2-0, the score 9-0 and Valentin significantly weaker from the right hand side, the shortstop was looking for just one pitch.

"I was looking dead red fastball and he threw me a change 2 and 0. Even with the score 9-0, nobody on base, he threw me a changeup. That's how crazy it is."

What started as a game, of course, has now turned into a beating. Clemens pitches 4⅔ innings, gives up seven hits, nine earned runs while walking four and striking out five. By contrast, Esteban Loiaza, who will finish second in this season's Cy Young voting to Toronto's Roy Halladay, is as commanding as Clemens is ineffective. The right-hander throws seven innings of shutout ball, yielding just one hit while striking out nine before leaving the game with a 9-0 lead.

In the top of the eighth, left-hander Gabe White, making his first appearance in a Yankee uniform, becomes New York's fourth pitcher of the night. He hits Carl Everett, then gives up Paul Konerko's second home of the game for an 11-0 White Sox lead. And Jose Valentin steps into the box for his final at-bat of the evening.

"I just go up there with no plan at all," he says. "I got a pitch to hit, and I missed it. Then he threw me a 3-2 breaking ball, and I swung and he strike me out." He shrugs.

"It's a 3-2 count, 11-0, one out, nobody on base, and I never think he was going to throw me a 3-2 slider. I mean, come on. He threw me a slider and strike me out. I was pissed. I was pissed not only because I strike out, but I think he was kind of scared to throw the fastball."

Tony Graffanino will pinch-hit for Roberto Alomar and stay in to play second. Willie Harris will replace Carl Everett and Scott Schoeneweis comes in to pitch the New York eighth. After striking out the first two batters Schoeneweis allows three straight hits, the last a two-run single by Derek Jeter, and the Yankees are on the board.

But this game is over. In the top of the ninth Magglio Ordonez parks a 3-2 offering from Antonio Osuna over the center field wall for his second home run of the game, the White Sox sixth of the contest, and makes the final score 13-2.

The visitor's locker room opens to media at 10:18. Outside the door, spikes from each of the White Sox players and coaches line the hallway for an overnight polish. Except for the lack of carpeting, and an out-of-place pair of catcher's shinguards thrown into the mix, this could be the club floor of the New York Palace hotel.

Inside the latest Busta Rhymes disc, *It Ain't Safe No More*, plays, loudly, on the clubhouse stereo. Most players are already down to shorts and T-shirts, digging in to full plates of post-game pasta. Except for Roberto Alomar. The second baseman is already showered, dressed, and on his way out the door, cup in hand, unwilling to wait for the team bus back to the hotel, unwilling to be cornered by the gathering beat writers.

Jose Valentin, too, is already showered. He sits in front of his locker to dress. He's got an early day tomorrow. His wife is leaving town.

5TH

Up the Middle

First Day on the Job

Getting to the big leagues. That was a dream. Once I got there I said, Now if I can just stay a year. Then when I got there a year I said, I'm going to try for two. At that time you had to vest four years to get the pension, and my goal was to get four years. And then I started playing. I started doing pretty good, and I went to five and six, and then obviously when you start playing and you're a regular your goal is to wear a ring. I got close a lot, in '75, '76, '77, '78. Came up short, and then to see it all come together in '80 is something that you can tell your players and you can relate to, but until you've been through it, been through the parade and get the ring, it's an experience you never forget because you look back at all the hard work and you look back and you say, Man, that was worth it.

— *Larry Bowa*

My first game when I played I looked at all the people in the stands, something like thirty, forty thousand people, and it was disappointing because I'm like an actor on a stage. In baseball, there's not any difference in the minors or in the sandlot. It's the same group of guys, same ball, same strike zone. It's just the quality of players are better, and a lot of them aren't as good in the majors as they are in the minors. The difference is you've got to have the right break, somebody really pushing you, because there's not that many Willie Mayses out there or Mickey Mantles. And so in a way, once you made it, it wasn't that big a deal to me. I mean, it was great. I still loved it. But it wasn't any different except the people. It's an attitude, a perception.
— *Jack Kubiszyn*

The first game I ever played in my life at shortstop was in the major leagues. We went to spring training, and spring training was in Havana in '53. After we signed we went back to New Jersey and visited a day with my dad and then we were in Havana. Pittsburgh signed three bonus players that year—[my brother] John, myself, and Vic Janowicz who was a catcher. We all ended up at spring training. It was then [Branch] Rickey told us he had planned on making a double play combination out of us. So, obviously for me, never having played in the infield at all, I had to start all over. When we started out he had me at second and John at short because John had played there, but I had a stronger arm and John made the double play better so he switched us. And then I went to short and they would hit me groundball after groundball after groundball because I was so used to the two and a half steps and release in the outfield where it's one and a half in the infield. So I was learning. The first time I ever played shortstop was against the Phillies. We played at Forbes Field and I pinch-hit against Robin Roberts, and then I went in the game and played shortstop. So I got to play that season. That team was a group of real old guys and real young guys. And they went with what they thought was the best to win early, and then once it showed it wasn't going to happen, they let John and myself play and we played 89 games in 1953.

— *Eddie O'Brien*

My first game was in Philadelphia. Curt Simmons was pitching, and the first time up I got a base hit. Then in the field I got a double play ball and Stan Lopata slid in and spiked me, and I played like I think two innings and they took me out because of the spike wound. It was my fault because I just stood there. I threw the ball to complete the double play and just stood there like a dummy and when he slid in he just happened to nick me.

— *Joe Koppe*

We had an exhibition game against the parent club. They always came into Tacoma on their way to San Francisco. Don Kessinger was on his two-week military duty, so they probably thought, Well, let's just drag him along because it's not that far. It's not that expensive. So they took me. I was there for three games and played one. It was probably just a look-see, and once we left San Francisco they sent me back to Tacoma. Which was good. I had no business being there. I wasn't going to play. My first major league game is in San Francisco, Candlestick Park, the ugliest night ballpark there could be. And I was freezing to death, but it never dawned on me how cold it was until I went back with Houston the next year. I thought, No wonder I couldn't play baseball here. It's like playing in a refrigerator. But I'll tell you what. There was Ron Santo and Fergie Jenkins and Glenn Becker and Billy Williams and Johnny Callison, Jim Hickman. That was one of the most fantastic groups of people you could ever be around. I got to meet them. Ernie Banks. It was wonderful. Yes, you put on the Cub uniform and it meant a lot, but when I left Tacoma to play in San Francisco I never expected to stay there. I knew it was just for a cup of coffee and so it didn't bother me. Plus, I didn't want to miss my trip to Hawaii. I mean, if you could play in Hawaii or Candlestick, where would you rather play?

— *Roger Metzger*

I remember when I first got called up in '80, Earl Weaver just looked at me and he said, "I don't care what the front office wants." The front office sent a letter to him to put me in the lineup, because I was going to be the shortstop. Ripken was going to be the third baseman. That's the way it was in the minor leagues. So Weaver calls me in his office and starts cussing me out and saying, "I'm the manager. I make out the lineup." And I said, "I'm just happy to be here. I hope I can help the team." So basically I just sat the bench. I entered into Earl's domain. He hates rookies and he doesn't want to be told what to do. I didn't do anything. It was cold in Toronto. It was wet. And somebody got hurt. He pinch-hit. We went into extra innings. Eddie Murray hit his third home run. We're winning 3-2 in like the twelfth or thirteenth, whatever it was, and then all of a sudden Earl stands up and he goes, Bonnicker, Bonnicker. And we don't know if he wants Boddicker or he wants me because we both got called up at the same time. So basically I went in the game, and the first ball that was hit to me was a rocket on wet AstroTurf that skipped right by me. I never got a glove on it. So then Earl cussed me out again.

— *Bobby Bonner*

The first game was 1964. The Dodgers had swept the Yankees in the World Series in '63, but in '64 things kind of went bad and they were out of it. I came in early August and got to play with them a whole month. I was playing every day. [Maury] Wills, when I first got there, had some kind of a problem and he was out for about a week and I played every game at short. Then when he came back I moved over to third, but I was playing every game, and I was loving it. I got a hit against the Phillies and beat them. You know, that was one of their big downfalls. The next night Willie Davis stole home in the bottom of the sixteenth, beat them 1-0. From then on

The SHORTSTOP

they were sliding right on out of it. They had a six-game lead when they came into LA.
— *Bart Shirley*

It was late September and there were five of us that came up from Minneapolis, and we reported to the Giants in the Polo Grounds. And the entrance in the Polo Grounds is out in right center field, way out there by the bullpen, so we all walked onto the field, and the clubhouse is out in deep centerfield up some stairs, so they all went on up to the clubhouse, and I just kind of stood there for about five minutes and looked around because I had to reminisce. My dad died when I was a sophomore in high school and, of course, he got me interested in baseball and the Cardinals and tears came to my eyes and I just thought, Boy, I wish my dad was here to see that I made it. I said, If I don't do anything, I've got to the big leagues. And of course that was a childhood dream like it is most kids.
— *Daryl Spencer*

My first game was in Cleveland in the old Municipal Stadium and it was dadgum 35 degrees and sleeting and raining all at once. It was a pretty good crowd the first day, but then after that it was about 3000 people. Gosh, it was weird just being in Cleveland.
— *Bill Spiers*

That's a special day. That's what you try to do your whole life, and then to be able to do it to where your folks can come to the game and so forth, that adds a lot to it. Even though I went 0 for 4, I still played well. Tried my best, hustled on and off the field, and it was quite a thrill. That ballpark back then at Anaheim Stadium was still brand new, and Gene Autry was the owner, and he had his own box up there where he could entertain guests. He had his own restaurant so after the games he could entertain guests and have dinner and so forth. But he would make the trip down after each game, and I can remember one time I was fortunate enough to have the game-winning hit, and he came in and he slipped me a hundred-dollar bill. And he called me "Kid." "Here, Kid, take your girlfriend out and have a good steak on me." That's the type of guy he was. He was just phenomenal.

— *Bruce Christensen*

Getting out on the field for the first time in the big leagues is pretty cool. Of course, you've been in spring training and you've played these other teams and a lot of these guys, but still I had not had a lot of experience. I remember sitting there thinking, Well, this is why they call it The Show. There's stuff happening. There's people all over the place. There's pageantry. There's pre-game ceremonies. It's just an assault on your senses when you first get there.

— *Paul Zuvella*

That was the greatest thrill of my life, I guess. We played Baltimore, and Bill White, a left-hander, was pitching,

Opening Day in Boston, and my first at-bat I got a base hit between third and short, which I'll never forget, and the second time I got a base hit off Skinny Brown between third and short. I had two base hits that day. We won. We beat Baltimore 8-4 or something.

— *Don Buddin*

It was an unbelievable thrill to put on a major league uniform. I owe everything in the world that I have to baseball.

— *Dick Groat*

The First Home Run

I can remember it because the guy I hit it off of—I want to say his name's [Bill] Fischer but I'm not sure—I played against in Triple A ball, and I don't think I ever hit a pop up against him. But I think, if I remember right, Dick Donovan was our pitcher, and it was a 1-0 game, I think. I hit the home run to win the game. But it was just a game. It was nice, but I didn't have any extra thrill.

— *Jack Kubiszyn*

Hit it off Paul Foytack in Detroit. 1956. It was a fastball.

— *Don Buddin*

I hit it off of Carl Erskine. It was in Brooklyn in 1953. It was my rookie year with the Giants, and to this day I'm the only middle infielder in the National League to hit 20 home runs or more in their rookie year. I think Ernie

Banks had 19. Ron Hansen and Joe Gordon and four or five guys have done it in the American League, but I'm the only National Leaguer to do that. So that kind of made my rookie year.

— *Daryl Spencer*

It was in the Astrodome. They had the shorter fences up, and the following year they moved the fences even farther back, which I never understood, but it was still pretty good. The ball never carried in the Dome very well at all. But I hit it off Bo McLaughlin. Yep, that was my first major league home run. And it was good that there was a fence because it didn't go in the stands, so I was able to get the ball back.

I didn't know it was gone when I hit it. I knew I hit it real well, but the first time, until you've done it, you're never quite sure. Not that I did it a lot anyway. But it was a fastball, middle in. You don't forget that. And I hit it down the left field line. I kind of pulled it, and it was pretty towering. I hit it well but I hit it real high.

— *Bill Almon*

I hit three home runs and one of them was a grand slam. Let's see. The first one was off John Tudor. They're all off left-handers. And I think the second one was the grand slam. That was off of Mike Caldwell. Then I hit one off Floyd Bannister of the White Sox in Chicago. Yeah, I had three home runs. I wasn't a power hitter.

— *Mike Fischlin*

I was in Triple A the first half of the year, and I just kind of found the power stroke or whatever after all those years, and I had ten home runs in Triple A at the All-Star break. I would hit five or six home runs in a year normally, but I had ten home runs at the All-Star break. It was off of Charlie Hough's knuckleball. When I hit it I said, Gosh, I hit that one pretty good. It felt like the ones I'd hit in Triple A, so it didn't surprise me when it went out. But I'll tell you this, it didn't take me long to get around those bases. I ran around the bases pretty quickly when I hit my first home run.

— *Paul Zuvella*

Traded
The Cubs were trying to make a run in '70 and they got Pepitone from Houston trying to make that last, late run, and I was the player to be named later. It was the greatest thing that ever happened to me. From that point on I was in the big leagues.

— *Roger Metzger*

It never hurt my feelings. It's kind of a letdown, but it doesn't hurt your feelings. Hey, you want to play ball? You like playing ball? Go play ball. Ain't no big deal. For me, hey, I'm just glad for the opportunity to be playing baseball. Go play.

— *Larvell Blanks*

A shortstop is what I was going to be, and really the only thing that changed it is Ozzie Smith. It's one of those being in the right place at the right time, or the wrong place at the wrong time type of situations, but my perspective on it was you always had to go out and produce. If they were going to move me for some reason, you can at least look back and say, Well, it wasn't for some flash in the pan. You give them credit. They saw an exceptional talent and they went with it.

— *Bill Almon*

(Being traded was) not really a surprise, just a hurt. I grew up as a Pirate fan and it'd been my whole life. I'd spent my whole career with the Pirates. Ironically it turned out to be the best thing that ever happened to me. I spent the three happiest years I ever spent in baseball in a Cardinal uniform.

— *Dick Groat*

The Career Highlight
I'd been wanting to pitch forever. That was my favorite position growing up. Love to pitch, but not a whole lot of 5'8" pitchers in the league. That wasn't even an option. But I think like a pitcher sometimes. I throw like a pitcher. I warm up. I work on my changeup. And it just so happens, we're getting blown out in a game, and [manager] Bobby Valentine came down to the end of the bench and was like, "Hey, when's the last time you pitched?" I said, "I don't know. It's been probably ten years ago. But I've got pretty good stuff." Bobby laughed. Todd Zeile was sitting right next to me, so Bobby asked Todd, "Hey, what do you got? What can you

do?" And Todd said, "I can throw some knuckleballs." I looked at Bobby like, Come on. You can't put this guy out there. I'm pretty legit. Just give me a shot. So he said, "All right, Des, you got the ball." I went to the pen and threw all my pitches for strikes and I felt really good. I got on the hill, and I felt like it was an American Legion game. It was just me and the catcher, and I had a whole lot of fun, man. Honestly it's my big league highlight. I got a big league inning, and got a strikeout. Hit 91 on the gun.

— *Desi Relaford*

'80 World Series, without a doubt. Not even close.

— *Larry Bowa*

LARRY BOWA

Honestly, I look back and think, How many people get a chance to play in the major leagues? How many people get a chance to stand out here on a baseball field and play against Pete Rose and Willie Mays and Hank Aaron and Ron Santo and Billy Williams and Ernie Banks and Tom Seaver and Steve Carlton and Bob Gibson? A lot of guys have single career moments, and the Gold Glove certainly was something I'm very proud of, but just the fact that you get to do something that you dream about and hundreds of thousands of other people dream about and don't get a chance to do. So, to me, it's probably no single moment. It's just being on the field with some of these people and all of the wonderful relationships you develop. Even though maybe you don't see each other for twenty years, and you happen to run into each other at an Old Timer's event or an airport or something, it's like you never missed a beat. Those are things you can't replace or single out. They're all very special.

— *Roger Metzger*

Playing with a lot of really good players and meeting a lot of really nice people. I mean, Dale Murphy sticks out for me. He was such a great guy, obviously a great competitor and quite a player, but here's a guy that just could never say no to anybody and was always very gracious signing autographs. There are people like that that you remember in the game and think, This is pretty cool. When you're young and coming up with the Braves you remember guys that helped you along—

105

Glen Hubbard and the Gene Garbers of the world. Good people that kind of teach you the ropes. Chris Chambliss is a great guy. A lot of really good people. Of course, you get traded to the New York Yankees and then you're sitting in the Yankees clubhouse with all these guys, your Dave Winfields and Don Mattinglys. Of course, I played against Mattingly a bunch coming up through the minor leagues, so it wasn't as big a thing, but I guess when you stop and realize, Wow, I'm in pinstripes, and this is really where it all began, that was kind of neat. That was kind of fun.

— *Paul Zuvella*

I guess what sticks out is the ability to play shortstop every day that second half of the season I hit .268. Being able to transition myself from the guy that was supposed to be the shortstop for the Astros for the next ten years and fell on his face to the guy that resurrected to being an everyday player with Dave Garcia in '82. That's probably the highlight for me. It was something for me to prove to myself that I could be an everyday ballplayer on the big league level. And it took me that long—from '77, back and forth from the minor leagues.

— *Mike Fischlin*

Personally, it was getting the game-winning hit in the '98 playoffs against Trevor Hoffman and the Padres, but team-wise it was winning our first division. That was something that I hadn't done until I got to Houston and that was just an unbelievable feeling, to clinch the division. Another thing was being part of Robin Yount's 3000th hit. And just playing with him was such a privilege. Being a part of that 3000th hit and seeing 55,000 flashbulbs go off every pitch before he got that hit was just unbelievable. It's something that'll just stick with you.

— Bill Spiers

The Toughest Play
Without a doubt the play in the hole, the backhand play. That's the toughest play because you're going to your right, you've got to plant, you've got to get rid of the ball, and if there's a guy that can run, obviously, it's all in one motion and it's tough.

— Larry Bowa

Ball in the hole. Another tough play is the slow-hit ball. Those balls are tough because you're fairly deep and when that ball hits, you've got to be moving. You can't delay at all. You have to be moving quickly, and while you're moving you'd better time it so that when you're catching that ball and that right foot's hitting—boom— you unload it.

— Alex Grammas

Deep in the hole. You've got to make a backhand play. You've got to make a perfect throw. That's got to be the toughest play.

— Bill Spiers

On a slow hit ball you have to come in to the infield grass and pick it up barehanded, kind of like a third baseman on a bunt play. But the play behind second base, a lot of times on TV they make that out like that's a great play, but that's a very simple play. Hell, you're going towards first base anyhow. But the play in the hole. I'm amazed at the arms. I had a pretty good arm, but some of these shortstops now are unbelievable.
— *Daryl Spencer*

I think the toughest play is the ball hit right at you.
— *Larvell Blanks*

The one hit right at you is the one you have problems with. You have no chance to adjust to it. You want to charge the ball most of the time, but when that ball's really stung at you, you have to take the hop you get.
— *Dick Groat*

How Pitchers Affect a Shortstop
I got along with pitchers just great. I could work with just about all of them. One of my big assets was knowing the guys that had the good moves, and we could work pick off plays or know when to go in to talk to them. Of course, at the big league level I didn't get a chance to do a lot of that, but Drysdale and I got along good. For a big man he could really turn on a dime and he loved to help himself out of jams. Of course, Koufax was different. He could care less about a base runner. He focused on those hitters. And he could get them. You learn their

strong suits. Drysdale liked to bore that ball in on right-handers and more than likely they were going to be hitting it your way or third base way towards the hole and you kind of shaded that way.

— *Bart Shirley*

With a sinkerball pitcher, you know the ball's going to be on the ground a lot. Other guys that keep the ball up a little more, you get more fly balls. You get some guys that are overpowering and with a lot of right-handers in the lineup you don't get as many balls your way.

— *Don Buddin*

When I was playing shortstop, the third baseman was Ken McMullen, and I gave him every pitch that was coming to a hitter. I gave the left fielders and the center fielders the pitches, so everybody knew what was coming, and I'd do it in different ways in case the opposing team says, "He's doing this all the time a curveball's coming" or whatever. We'd mix it up, the signs, or what I would do. This really helped us out as a team. If you know a pitch and a location, that's half the battle on defense, and you can adjust and cheat. Guys like Andy Messersmith, Clyde Wright, Rudy May. We would sit down before the game, and I don't care if we were playing the Yankees or Boston or whatever, we would go down the whole starting lineup and they would explain how they would like to pitch to every hitter in every different type of situation.

— *Bruce Christensen*

You watch how the pitcher pitches the guy. You see how the guy's swinging the bat. You've seen him play before. You know where he likes to hit the ball. You keep all of that in your head, and you add your instinct to that, based upon how a guy may be swinging lately or how the pitcher seems to be throwing. Maybe he's got a little more zip on his fastball or whatever. Tom Candiotti was a teammate of mine in Cleveland. He would like to sit with me before games and say, "Okay, Zu, here's where this guy likes to hit this off of me." Because obviously Tom was a knuckleballer and he's different. How do you defense a knuckleballer? But he knew. He knew how guys liked to do it and when I first got up to Cleveland he'd sit with me and we'd talk. With George Brett he'd said, "I want you way over in the hole." And so I'd be way over in the hole, and he'd kind of look at me and just kind of flip his glove. Get over there more, you know. And sure enough that guy didnhit the ball right to me a couple of times. But that's the kind of hitter George Brett was. He's going to wait and wait and wait on that ball and hit it the other way into the hole.

— *Paul Zuvella*

You have to learn hitters and learn how to play them. You have to think in this game. You have to know the hitters, every one of them, and know how they're going to react to Chris Short and to Jim Bunning and how they're going to play. You'd better have some idea, every hitter on every opposing team, how you want to play them and where you think you should be. Baseball's a game of percentage. You know what kind of stuff pitchers on your own staff have and how they're going to pitch everybody, and obviously, you become a better shortstop the better pitchers you have. When they say they're going to pitch a guy a certain way, they pitch him that way.

— *Dick Groat*

Strengths and Weaknesses

If it was hit in my area, I got you. I got you. Which is going to be 90 percent of the time anyway. The thing to me is to catch the balls that are hit to you, in your range, and throw them out. Control. Accuracy. I never had too much trouble with accuracy. I always felt like I could play with a blind first baseman. That's not to say I never made a bad throw, but basically he wouldn't have any trouble catching a ball that I threw him. If anything, if he was that bad, I would probably feel sorry for him. That'd tighten me up. I was worried because he's probably worried.

— *Alex Grammas*

I had a good arm, a real good arm, and I could move quick and I could run pretty good.

— *Joe Koppe*

I could turn a double play, I think, with the best of them because of my arm. I could always put a little extra on it and get that man at first.

— *Bart Shirley*

I had range. Then overall, as a player, I could put the bat on the ball. Range. Average fielder. Average fielding shortstop.

— *Larvell Blanks*

I had pretty good hands, and I had pretty quick feet. I had a pretty good arm, but I didn't have the range that some of the guys do. But you know I was a smarter guy and I positioned myself well.

— *Paul Zuvella*

I had a lot of range and played defense really good, but I was also valuable to a team because I could play second, I could play third. But shortstop was my natural position, and I liked it the most. I loved that position. I miss it to this day.

— *Mike Fischlin*

I couldn't run a lick. I'm still looking for my second infield hit. I did not realize this until I was a senior in college, when the scouts were clocking me. I didn't have the greatest arm until I went to St. Louis, because I worked to develop it that winter because I hated Joe Brown for trading me. I did have a great arm from that point on. I worked all winter, changing my delivery. Everything I did was different when I went to St. Louis. I remember Ken Boyer telling me when I went in the hole and threw somebody out, he said, "I never thought you had an arm that good." And I said, "I didn't."

— *Dick Groat*

Sliders

Nobody slid harder into second base than Willie Mays and Frank Robinson. And you know the guys that slide the hardest when you're playing the infield, the middle infield. You know. They don't have to tell you. You know.

— *Alex Grammas*

Most people don't realize that Gil Hodges was one of the hardest sliders, and I don't think he's even mentioned when they talk about hard sliders. Of course, Frank Robinson, he was probably the worst as far as coming in spikes high. I became a pretty hard slider, and it really carried over in my career in Japan. I changed the whole structure of baseball running in Japan with my sliding. I never came in with my spikes high. I just had a knack of being able to take out the shortstop or second baseman. I got hit a lot of times, but I never said nothing. I just went out and did my job. When I got traded guys welcomed me aboard and said, "Just play hard like you did against us."

We had a play against Milwaukee one year. Johnny Logan was playing short and Mel Roach was playing second and there was a ground ball. I wasn't the fastest runner but I could go from first to third and score from second, and I could break up double plays. Well, Logan fumbled the ball, and Roach went to second base, and he had to hesitate and plant his foot to get Logan's throw. I slid in and broke his leg. But if Logan hadn't fumbled the ball, Roach would've made his little hop,

113

and I would've knocked him down and that would've been it. I think that's the only player that I ended up actually hurting, and it was the fact that Logan fumbled the ball.

— *Daryl Spencer*

If there's any one person that I thought about coming in there it would be Dave Winfield, just because of his size. He came in hard. Not that he did anything trying to take you out; it's just he's a big man coming in hard.

— *Bill Spiers*

[Gary] Matthews, without a doubt. Sarge. Nothing dirty, but you just knew that if he's coming down to second base, he's going to clean your clock.

— *Mike Fischlin*

Out of the Box
You played the hitter. For example, Richie Ashburn, he was like the Ichiro of our time. You had to really be up on him.

— *Eddie O'Brien*

Richie Ashburn. I'd play him really in, about four feet back behind the infield grass. He just got out of the box so quick that you had to play him really shallow.

— *Daryl Spencer*

Vada Pinson with the Cincinnati Reds.

— *Joe Koppe*

Bo Jackson was just one awesome specimen. You'd shorten up with him. Deion Sanders. Kenny Lofton. All those guys that could fly, and especially left-handed hitters that kind of slapped it. Oh yeah, you would shorten up tremendously.

— *Bill Spiers*

Left-handed little slap hitters that could absolutely fly. Otis Nixon comes to mind for me because I played against him in the big leagues, and I played against him in the minor leagues, in Triple A, so I played many a game against him, and he had one foot out of the box as he was making contact with the ball, and he could flat out fly. He could also push a bunt your way. And Tony Fernandez ran really well. Not like an Otis Nixon but still very well, and you got to know after playing with those guys awhile that, yeah, I'd cheat the other way, and I'd cheat in, and if they hit the ball up the middle past me, oh well. You tried to take the hitter out of his strength and make him adjust to where you were playing. In other words, if Nixon's strength or Fernandez's strength was to try and slap the ball through the hole, then you'd shade him that way. You'd shade him in a little bit and make him try and hit it by the pitcher, and maybe he wasn't quite as adept at doing that.

— *Paul Zuvella*

Oh my God, [Mickey] Mantle. Well, you didn't want to get too close on Mantle, but you had to.

— *Don Buddin*

115

The Playing Fields

The Polo Grounds was the best infield. That and Cincinnati were the two best infields. Those two groundskeepers were brothers. I used to love to play in the Polo Grounds because the infield was so good. Eddie Stanky would say, "You never miss a ball in this ballpark, do you?" And I said, "You know, I feel that way." He said, "I know. I can tell by watching you." The texture was perfect and you could cover up the indentation from your spikes and stuff so easy, and you very seldom got bad bounces. When we'd go to Philadelphia and play at Shibe Park, a lot of times they'd have dust that thick. You'd come out of there and you'd be black from here down from where you would sweat in the summer. It was horrible. That type of field was the toughest, because it changes the speed of the ball. You're looking for something hard and that takes a little of the speed off. The timing gets off just a little bit. In Brooklyn you'd get a lot of bad hops. If a field was real bad, I might shorten up just a little bit to not give the ball another bounce. Unless they had a guy on second where you wanted to knock the ball down. You had to try to knock the ball down if you couldn't throw the guy out. Then you'd change, but for ordinary hitters, if the field was that slow, I would shorten up. Cincinnati's infield was cut very deep, and I would never play at the edge of the grass. It was too deep. Smooth field, but deep, and you'd give yourself less chance of throwing somebody out.

— *Alex Grammas*

Ebbets Field had a beautiful infield. There wasn't a pebble on it. The Polo Grounds had kind of a whitish sand feel to it. Crosley Field in Cincinnati sloped backwards at the back end of the infield. The Cardinals in St. Louis, it was like playing on brick. The field was so burnt out the ball goes like it does on AstroTurf today. Pittsburgh was a little bit difficult because the field for some reason was fairly hard between short and third, in that section, but kind of sandy up the middle, so the ball would come up to your right but would stay down to your left. So there were different little nuances in the parks.

We were playing in Milwaukee and County Stadium one Sunday afternoon, and a ground ball off the bat, usually you can pick up where it's going, and I started to go up the middle, and the ball went between short and third, and it came out of the white shirts. I lost it immediately. Johnny Logan was the Milwaukee shortstop, and as we were coming off the field he yelled over to me, "Don't worry about it, O'B. I've done it six or seven times already this year." When the ball was hit, it had a tendency to come out, if there were white shirts back there, and you could actually lose the ground ball. On Sunday afternoon, a lot of the white shirts were there. Cleveland was terrible. Cleveland had grass like three inches in the infield. You couldn't hit the ball through there, unless they hit a one-hopper. If they hit a ground ball, hell, they were out, because it was slow.

I think Shibe Park in Philly was kind of an ugly park. I would say Shibe Field was the worst. I went over in the hole once. The ball hit something and come up, and

I've still got scar in my chin where it hit me, and it ended up they gave me an error. I had to get two stitches in my face.

— *Eddie O'Brien*

I always loved playing at Wrigley Field. That was probably my favorite baseball park. You walk into that field, and it was baseball. It was just what you dreamed of. Houston and St Louis had AstroTurf and a dirt infield when I first came up, and that was just horrendous. Those were treacherous ballparks, but then they turfed everything and only made the little cuts around second and first and third. That was a little bit more relief. To me, baseball was meant to be played on grass and dirt. Anytime the ball skips from the Turf to the dirt it puts a new spin on it. AstroTurf accelerated the speed of the ball. So you have the ball spinning and it develops a top spin once it comes off of that and hits the dirt. After my '71 season, they closed up and they put Turf all around the field except for the base cutouts, but the number of balls that hit in there, you just had to deal with it. It wasn't like it happened all the time, but you still had to make some adjustments.

— *Roger Metzger*

St. Louis had the worst infield I ever played on. It took so many bad hops. There was just not a good true bounce. It was awful. Kansas City had a great infield. I loved to play in Kansas City. It was beautiful.

— *Don Buddin*

I thought Dodger Stadium was a tough place to play. They had hard red dirt when I was there. I think they brought in some off-color dirt later on. But it was hard, packed hard. You get some tricky hops when you have hard ground like that.

— *Bart Shirley*

The grass part of infields would determine where you played position-wise because some teams had it thicker than others. Wrigley Field used to have thicker grass. Some of your teams had the real shaved grass, and it was faster, almost like AstroTurf. Tiger Stadium had real thick grass. A lot of times teams did that because of their pitching situation. If you had a lot of groundball/sinker type pitchers they'd want high grass. Or soft dirt right in front of the plate. That was very common to see. If you saw real soft dirt right in front of the plate you knew a sinkerball pitcher was pitching.

— *Bill Spiers*

A lot of guys liked playing on turf. I did not. Number one, you had seams involved and, number two, if a guy hit a ball with topspin off the bat, by that second hop it would gain speed. It actually picked up speed and created almost an overspin. So it took a little getting used to. Minnesota was tough because Minnesota had a very bouncy turf. Cincinnati, by the time I was playing there, had some pretty nasty seams. Dodger Stadium was a neat place. It was a fun place. But the dirt there wasn't the best. Remember those years with Russell and Lopes

119

and Garvey and all those guys and they'd have a bunch of errors? Well, you know, that wasn't the easiest field to field on. At Candlestick you had to deal with the wind and the dirt wasn't the best. Atlanta could get chopped up a little bit. As a shortstop, that's always how you measured the field—how is the dirt?
— *Paul Zuvella*

Candlestick in San Francisco—that thing was like playing on a rock. And there were seams and it was hard and it was fast. I'm telling you, you can get some tough topspin hops on turf.
— *Mike Fischlin*

I guess the worst I ever played on was in the Astrodome because it was under a roof and it was just chopped up. They had a very bad mix.
— *Dick Groat*

The Double Play
Lew Burdette slid in out in San Francisco and tore my pants up. I've got a picture of me walking off the field. I went in the clubhouse and changed pants, but it didn't hurt me.

You learn early, if you keep your feet planted you're going to get hurt, so you've got to have a little jump. If you just get a quarter of inch off the ground, your feet will go out from under you but you'll fall on the ground. What I used to do when a guy would come in after me, I'd get up and my first step would be a step right on his

chest. You just had to get the respect of the players. And they appreciated that.
— *Daryl Spencer*

Of course, you get hit at short a lot, but this one time [my brother] John backhanded me the ball, and he hung it. It was like a pop fly and I got hit by Ted Kluszewski. I went flying back past the bag, and Kluszewski, he was ready for it. You knew everybody in those days. We played everybody 22 times, 11 in, say, Ebbets Field and 11 in Forbes. And there were only eight teams so you knew all the players who played year in and year out. So Kluszewski said, "You can't blame me for that one. That one's John's fault." And he was right.
— *Eddie O'Brien*

A lot of times you got your clock cleaned pretty good, but you had everything in front of you, so you had a good feel. You didn't necessarily see the runner, but you could feel him or hear him. A lot of it is just feel, being light on your feet. Most shortstops are. They know how to fall. So you square off for the throw and you make your relay and then you get up as soon as you possibly can. If it is a quarter of an inch off the ground then fine, let them take your legs out. You can tumble, but you know how to fall and you're going to be fine. But if you're sitting there turning and planting your front leg, and they're hitting your front leg as you're throwing, then you're in trouble. But you clear yourself out, and if you've got to kick yourself out three feet toward right field, you do that. If it takes you a split second longer to relay, oh well. You've got to take care yourself, so you can live to turn another double play.

— *Paul Zuvella*

Make them get down. Because if they're going to come get me, I'm going to come get them. I'm going to throw right at their head, and they'll slide then. Because that's just the only protection I have. And any shortstop will probably tell you that. That part of the game never bothered me because I knew it was part of the game. I hung in there good, and I'd take my licks. You do it for the team. You do it for your pitcher out there. You're trying to win. You're trying to compete.

— *Mike Fischlin*

Ouch

I blew out a disc in my back the last home game of '91. I was sliding, trying to break up a double play. In fact, I didn't start that game. I'd come in, pinch-run or something, and when I slid I just kind of slid awkwardly I guess, and a disc popped out of my back. It just happened. I was really swinging the bat good. That was my third year, and I was having a pretty decent year, and I went ahead and played the rest of the games that year. I remember finishing up in Boston and being in such pain with my back, but I kept playing just because I was swinging the bat good, and I wanted to finish up strong. Then I rested awhile and then had it checked and they said you need surgery if you're going to play next year.

Then the process started. You don't ever know what's going to happen, and I can't complain one bit about my career because I ended up loving what I did in Houston, playing as a utility guy. I really enjoyed that more than just being a shortstop. It affected me playing shortstop. There's no doubt about that.

— *Bill Spiers*

I got beaned by Jim Bunning in 1960. It was a fastball. Second game of a doubleheader. It knocked the visor off. I was unconscious. I had to go to Santa Maria, and I was there for a few days. Had concussions and all that good stuff. I came back and I tried to play. It's very difficult. I never got over that, I'm sure. I've still got an indentation in my forehead, right dead center. I can stick my finger up there now and feel it. It was an extra-inning game, and Earl Wilson had just hit a double off him. I fouled a couple off down the left field line, hit pretty good. And he was throwing to knock me down, really. And I ducked into the ball instead of away from it. I just lost it. And when I did it just came in on me. It went right through the front of my helmet and put a hole in my head. I never will forget. Frank Sullivan came out there. I can remember that. He said, "My God, he's got a hole in his head."

— *Don Buddin*

6TH

Cup of Coffee Shortstops

F eel free to pick your historical moment here, but between 1945 (the last year that the Chicago Cubs participated in a World Series, as well as the end of World War II which, among other benefits, allowed major league rosters to return to nearly full strength with the return of veterans from the service) and the year 2000, thirty-two men fulfilled their boyhood dream of playing in the major leagues. Yet their dreams were abbreviated, with career big league appearances totaling in the mere single digits.

There have been players who briefly touched the position of major league shortstop since 2000. Originally drafted in the seventh round of the 1995 draft, Mike Moriarty played eight games for the Baltimore Orioles, including four at shortstop, in 2002. He committed no errors in the field and managed a .188 batting average in 16 plate appearances. At season's end he was granted free agency and signed with the Toronto Blue Jays who released him in June of '03. One month later Moriarty had signed with the Astros, but once again garnered free agency at season's end without appearing in a major league game. He signed with the Rockies in December of '03, his third team in just over six months, but was released out of spring training the following season. In April of 2004 Moriarty signed with the Pirates organization and once again earned free agent status at the end of the season.

James Lofton, no relation to the Football Hall of Fame wide receiver, was selected by the Cincinnati Reds in the 1993 amateur draft. The Reds released Lofton at the end of 1997 and he drifted below organized baseball's radar for nearly four years when the Boston Red Sox signed him away from the independent Western League's Sonoma County Crushers in June of 2001. Lofton made his major league debut the following September and appeared in eight games for Boston, collecting an RBI and two stolen bases. But the rookie made two errors in the field for a fielding percentage of just .920 with a batting average of .192. Lofton stayed with the Red Sox organization for another year and a half before being released. He's since spent time with Nashua, managed by former Red Sox third baseman Butch Hobson, in the independent Northern League, as well as the Baltimore Orioles organization.

Both Jason Alfaro and Josh Labandeira made short-term debuts at shortstop during the 2004 season, though neither returned with the parent club in 2005. Labandeira, a sixth round draft pick of the Expos in 2001, made his major league debut on September 17, 2004, but went hitless in 14 at-bats. He split his 2005 season between the Double A Harrisburg Senators and the Triple A New Orleans Zephyrs. Jason Alfaro, a 22nd round draft pick of the Astros in 1997, made his major league debut with Houston on September 9, 2004 and collected his first big league hit off Pittsburgh's Josh Fogg in his first at-bat after he'd entered the second game of a doubleheader as a defensive replacement. Alfaro spent all of 2005 with the Syracuse SkyChiefs of the International League where he batted .247 with 10 home runs over 105 games.

But recent, happier stories exist.

Eddie Rogers, one of 66 major leaguers born in San Pedro de Macoris, Dominican Republic, signed with the Baltimore Orioles as an amateur free agent in 1997. By 2002, Rogers had made his major league debut with the club, though he went hitless in his three at-bats. But Rogers returned to the majors in 2005, appearing in eight games for the Orioles, primarily as a pinch-runner. In fact, such was the overwhelming use of Rogers as a pinch-runner that Eddie scored four runs for Baltimore despite only coming to the plate once. But on September 26, 2005, in his only at-bat of the season and with his team trailing 11-0 in the ninth inning, Eddie Rogers hit a two-run homer off the Yankees' Alan Embree for his first major league hit. Rogers was optioned back to Ottawa at season's end.

Jason Bartlett was taken in the 13th round of the 2001 draft by the San Diego Padres and sent to the Minnesota Twins, in exchange for Brian Buchanan, thirteen months later. Bartlett made his major league debut as a late-inning replacement with Minnesota on August 3, 2004, and struck out against Matt Hensley during the Twins' 10-0 whitewashing of the Angels. But Bartlett collected his first major league hit, as well as his first RBI, against White Sox pitcher Jon Garland on September 21st of that season, and was in the starting lineup for the Twins on Opening Day of 2005. His 74 games played in 2005 permanently removed Bartlett from the Cup of Coffee rolls.

At least three more shortstops made abbreviated major league appearances in 2005 (more than three rookie shortstops came up during the season, but only three played the majority of their games in the field at the position). Danny Sandoval played in three games for the Phillies, Hanley Ramirez played in two for the Red Sox and Pedro Lopez managed two base hits and two RBI in his two games with the White Sox.

But enough of the young guys. What about those grizzled veterans of yesteryear? Can players of yesteryear truly be considered veterans if they're not, indeed, somewhat grizzled? Feel free to insert a Snoop Dogg, sizzle the fizzle on the grizzle joke here if you would like. Where were we? Oh yeah. What was the experience like for those thirty-two shortstop souls who managed but a brief glimpse of major league life between the Cubs' last World Series appearance and the turn of a new century?

When 18-year-old Perry Currin made his major league debut with the St. Louis Browns on June 29,

1947, he was the third-youngest player in the American League.

"I was torn between taking a scholarship to college or signing with the pros right out of high school," Currin says. "It was a tough decision because the statistics of people making it to the major leagues is pretty drastic. And if you have a college background you have something to back up to. But when I finished playing pro ball, I didn't have any college education. So I had to go to work for a living."

Currin signed with the Browns, and was given a major league contract for a $5000 bonus. And with it he bought a brand new blue Pontiac. After signing, Currin's first stop was St. Louis. "I went with the Browns right away," he says. "I went into St. Louis and traveled with them to New York, Philadelphia, Chicago, Boston. And then I was farmed out to Springfield, Illinois. I was in a couple ballgames, but that was about it."

Actually three. He played his first game in June. Just a month prior Perry Currin had been an Arlington, Virginia high school student. And for his debut appearance, Currin was called on to pinch-hit. Against a pitcher by the name of "Rapid Robert" Feller. The result of that meeting?

"I walked," says Currin.

But soon Currin was sent down to Springfield for some minor league seasoning.

"I was with the club for a while and then I went down and then they brought me back up when the minor league season was over. It was pretty exciting to tell you the truth," Currin says.

But there was the requisite nervousness involved for such a young man.

"All these guys were professional ballplayers," he says. "They've been in the big leagues for some time, and here I am up there trying to take their job."

Which is not to say that his Browns teammates were antagonistic.

"All the guys were very nice. I didn't have any derogatory feelings whatsoever about any of them."

Currin's manager, former catcher Muddy Ruel, practiced law in the off-season and is credited for first labeling the catcher's equipment "the tools of ignorance."

"He talked to me quite a bit," Currin says. "I sat beside him, and he was showing me the different ins and outs of major league baseball. It's a lot different up there than anywhere else."

Still, even with benefit of counsel from the counselor, a long-term career was not to be. Currin would play more baseball, but he'd never again reach the major leagues.

"The highlight," he says, "is being up there with people that really are successful, and doing something that not many people get a chance to do. And you meet a lot of nice people. I made a lot of friends and acquaintances in the minor leagues and in the big leagues. I met Joe DiMaggio and Ted Williams and those kind of guys.

"I met Ted Williams in Boston. We lived at a hotel close to the ballpark so I walked to the ballpark, and I walked out on the field early with just my pants and a sweatshirt on. And there was a guy at home plate casting a fishing rod towards second base. That was Ted Williams. I talked to him a few minutes. Watching him play and watching DiMaggio play and the way they hit that ball and everything else, it makes you a believer in the game."

For one who started so young, even a four-year pro career means that you're still young when you walk away.

"I had been in the minor leagues," Currin says, "and the Browns wanted me to go to Canada to manage and play for a team in Canada, and I didn't want to go. I had gotten married so I just figured it was time to give it up. But I really enjoyed it. I have very fond memories of the whole situation."

Though Al Naples wasn't quite as young as Perry Currin, he also managed a cup of coffee with the St. Louis Browns in the late 1940s. Naples grew up in New York City where his high school team won the city baseball championship, and despite playing shortstop cheered, in particular, for Yankee first baseman Lou Gehrig.

"He was quiet, kept to himself, and he just had a lot of good ethics about him. He was a hard worker, and I just liked watching him. He was my idol, I guess you'd say."

After graduating from St. Peters in 1944, Naples enlisted in the service. He served two years on a Naval destroyer, and then in 1946 entered Georgetown University on a basketball scholarship. But one sport would not be enough.

"I was fortunate to play baseball down there under Joe Judge who was an old-time Washington Senators first baseman, so he sort of groomed me. He was a really good coach."

After his junior year Naples got the opportunity to work out with several major league teams, including the Braves, Reds, and Senators.

"They would keep you housed up and you could go out and work with the players, and then you would sit in the stands and watch the game," he says. "But there was no scout that I can remember directly talking about wanting to sign you. I just got a phone call that summer from Bill DeWitt asking me if I wanted to sign with the Browns. I guess it was the middle of June, so I flew up to Boston and just negotiated a contract. The next day I played. I was getting, I think, $8,500, and guys like Carl Furillo, who had won World Series and everything else, were making the same amount, so it didn't make sense."

Naples started two consecutive games for the Browns and hit a double off of Red Sox pitcher Mel Parnell in his very first at-bat.

"Birdie Tebbetts was the catcher," Naples says. "I think he might have gone to a Jesuit school. They try to distract you, you know, and he said to me, Oh, a Jevvy boy. He said, Another one of those eggheads, or something to that effect. I can remember him talking to me and saying things like that.

"I think it went into right center," he says of his first

major league hit. "I keep thinking I could've had a triple on it, but the third base coach, I could see him holding me up."

Like Perry Currin two years before, Naples was sent down to Springfield, the Three-I League, to finish the year, and when his season was up he enrolled at Fordham to finish his college degree. His career as a professional ballplayer was effectively over.

"I got married that year," Naples says. "January of '50. I finished school that year. They wanted me to get in shape and they sent me down to a team in the Texas League. And we had a baby at that time so we took the baby and we went down there and we were living out of a hotel room and we were getting up at midnight or whatever, in the middle of the night, looking for milk. I went in and saw them after about three or four days of living this way. My daughter was sleeping in a bureau drawer. I told them that I was running out of money, and I wanted them to put me on the payroll, and they would not do that until they considered I was in shape. So I went home that day. I left. They put me on the restricted list, and I've been on the restricted list ever since."

Dick Barone's cup of coffee came with the team that would become the 1960 World Champion Pittsburgh Pirates. But it was a much longer road than either Perry Currin's or Al Naples' relative overnight jump to big leagues. The shortstop from just below California's Bay Area began his professional career in 1951.

"I played in Great Falls, Montana," Barone says. "I was signed to the Pittsburgh organization by Bob Fontaine. Out of high school. I was about 18. Money wasn't an object. I got $200 a month. I was just happy to be playing professional baseball."

His love of the game, of course, began earlier.

"My favorite team was the San Francisco Seals in the Pacific Coast League," he says. "I went to see a lot of games in Seals Stadium, and then when I was a senior in high school I was picked out of northern California to play in that game, the East-West game, in Seals Stadium. So that was a thrill. The catcher on our team was John McNamara."

Barone's professional career, however, would start at a lower level. Great Falls was in the Pioneer League. Class C ball. Just one step from the bottom of the minor league ladder. And the trip to the majors would take nine long years.

"I had about three or four major league contracts," Barone says, "but I'd be optioned out to Triple A. I played Triple A six years. International League for two years and the Pacific Coast League for four."

And though Triple A might seem close, just one tiny step away from the big leagues, Dick Barone suffered no illusions.

"I wasn't really waiting for a call from the parent club," he says, "because Dick Groat was there, and I was behind him all the time. I was hoping maybe a trade would come up. Every once in a while I'd hear things but they never materialized."

And for career minor leaguers, especially before the days of free agency, off-season work was a necessity to pay the bills.

At a certain point even staying put at the Triple A level feels like a step back. It feels like for every day you stay in place, the majors actually get further away. And thoughts of quitting come more frequently. Occasionally they take root and grow.

"The thing is," Barone says, "you always have that in back of your mind. Well, maybe this is the year it's going to happen. You always had that hope. That's why you stick in there. Then finally I quit when I was 30 years old," he says. "I was still in good shape, but I just figured it was time to get a regular job. Then, you know, 30 was older then than it is nowadays."

Of course, just because you feel old doesn't mean that quitting something you've done for more than half your life is easy.

"When spring training came around," he says, "you got that fever. And it was tough. It wasn't easy."

It still isn't.

"One year I went up to Scottsdale, Arizona, for vacation, and there was a new Triple A stadium at the time. And just that exhibition game and smelling that grass out there, boy, that was tough. It really brought back a lot of memories. I'm saying, 'What am I doing sitting here watching this game? I should be out there in a uniform, as a coach or a manager or something.'"

As tough as retirement was, it would certainly be tougher had Barone not made the majors. And that albeit short trip to the majors almost didn't happen.

"Groat got hurt and so I got the okay to go up there. Now I don't remember the date exactly. I really don't. They were in the pennant race naturally. They were an unbelievable team. Even though Groat was hurt they had Dick Schofield."

Barone was with Triple A Columbus when he got the summons.

"I believe it was my manager, Cal Ermer, who told me," Barone says. "And then our general manager. And I go, 'You're kidding me.' Because I didn't have too good a year that year. I got beat up a little bit. Broke a bone or whatever. It was just an off year."

Barone finally saw action in a major league as a pinch-runner on September 22, 1960.

"That was against Milwaukee. In Milwaukee. We clinched it that night. And so that was the celebration. We left Milwaukee and came into Pittsburgh."

In Pittsburgh, after the Pirates clinched the pennant, Barone got his first chance to start, yet went 0 for 5 against Reds' starter Bob Purkey. The game went 16 innings and ended in a 4-3 Pirates victory, but Dick Schofield came in as Barone's late-inning replacement.

"That's the way they were going then," Barone says. "They couldn't lose a game. It was amazing."

But Barone had one more chance against Milwaukee's Bob Buhl.

"That's the game I thought I had a hit. I hit it to right center and thought I was going to go for three. And Aaron made a shoestring catch. Anyway, that was

135

The SHORTSTOP

my shot for a base hit. That was the closest, because I can remember Murtaugh said, 'You ripped it good.'"

Of course, when playoff time came, when the Pirates headed to that fateful series against the vaunted New York Yankees, Dick Groat had returned and there was no place for a short-timer like Dick Barone on the roster.

"I stayed around for the first two games," he says. "I watched the first two games from the stands, and then went into the clubhouse after the game, and talked to some of the guys, and then I headed for home."

And that was the major league career. Not a lot of time for highlights, but Barone's baseball pride remains.

"The biggest thrill for me lately is my grandson got signed by the Marlins," he says. "Daniel Barone. He pitched for Greensboro in the Class A South Atlantic League. And we listen to him on the Internet and it's great. My wife and I just sit by that radio and listen to it."

Shortstop Bobby "Scroggy" Durnbaugh was born in Dayton, Ohio, grew up in Dayton, Ohio, and now lives in Dayton, Ohio. And in 1957 he was brought up, briefly of course, to play for his hometown (more or less) Cincinnati Reds. And though the Reds were, indeed, Durnbaugh's favorite team as a child, his favorite player wore a different uniform.

"He was everybody's favorite player. Ted Williams," says Durnbaugh. "You'd pick up a newspaper and you'd look and see how he did that day."

But about that nickname . . .

"Tommy Brown gave me that, and I have no idea where it come from. Just out of the blue one day he started it, and it kind of stuck there." Of course, veterans get to make the rules, even when they don't make any sense.

Durnbaugh began his professional ascent straight out of high school.

"We had to try out for the scouts," he says, "and the scouts approached me, and I signed and they sent me to Welch, West Virginia. That was Class D ball then."

The Cincinnati organization was the first to approach the young shortstop.

"Probably the first ones to make an offer," Durnbaugh says. "I talked to some Cleveland scouts and some Philadelphia Athletic scouts. But Cincinnati kind of stepped forward. My dad and I talked a little bit about it, and it didn't take us long to make up our mind that's what we wanted to do."

Durnbaugh's father also played baseball and occasionally gave his son advice on the game but didn't have the time to pursue the sport himself.

Shortstop had always been Durnbaugh's primary position.

"The coach put me there, and that's where I went," he says. "I liked it. Either shortstop or second base was much more suited for me than anyplace else. Probably my size more than anything. And if you don't hit the long ball you don't go to the outfield. So I would say short and second was probably where I was destined to be."

137

Durnbaugh's trek to the majors was a standard progression—D ball to C ball and on and on, until pretty soon six years have gone by and you're sitting at home, in Dayton, Ohio, following the 1957 minor league season. But little did Bobby Durnbaugh know that it was time for his dream to come true.

"I got a call from Gabe Paul at Cincinnati," he says. "They were home then, and I joined them in Cincinnati, and then we went to Milwaukee. It was just the end of the year, and you could bring up extra ballplayers. It was a courtesy call. They weren't planning on showcasing me. You've only got a week to go. They can't do too much. So I have no idea what prompted it, but I was appreciative."

From Dayton to Cincinnati, of course, is a short drive. So for a minor leaguer already home, prepared for another off-season, there would be no cross-country flights to meet his new team.

"My wife and I and my mom and dad all went to the ballgame, all went to Cincinnati," Durnbaugh says. "I drove back, and then we drove down the next day. I stayed at home, and we went back and forth until I went to Milwaukee."

The movie script, of course, would have Durnbaugh bat in that first game, perhaps lining a home run over the left field fence, and as he rounded third, catch a glimpse of his mother, father, and bride huddled together behind the home dugout, applauding through the tears of happiness at their son's, her husband's big league triumph. But in Durnbaugh's short career, a mere five-day stretch from his first major league appearance on September 22nd to his last on September 27th, in those meager two games with the Reds in 1957, he managed just one plate appearance. And it didn't happen at home.

It took place in County Stadium in Milwaukee where the soon-to-be World Champion Braves soon would host the powerhouse Yankees. And the pitcher he faced?

"Lew Burdette," Durnbaugh recalls. "He knew how to throw the ball. He knew where to throw the ball. He didn't get much of the white part. He was on the edges all the time. I grounded out to shortstop."

The game against Milwaukee, the game that would be Durnbaugh's last in the majors, also contained a fielding error.

"I talked to George Crowe about it later on," Durnbaugh says, "and he said the ball was there in time. He said, 'You got a bad call on that, Bobby.' And that was it. But I accepted the error, you know. It didn't hurt my career."

Durnbaugh laughs at the recollection, then goes on to explain.

"Felix Mantilla was running. Nobody says anything to you, and I was too dumb to ask anybody, but he ran better than I thought he did. It was a slow hit ball, and I had to step it up a notch. The ball got up and away a little bit, but big old George Crowe grabbed him. Well, anyway, that's the way it went."

Durnbaugh returned to the minors in 1958 and 1959. By 1960 he'd had enough and returned home to

139

Dayton.

"I decided that I wasn't going to go anyplace, and it's time to get busy and do something," he says. But a year later he got a call from Ernie White, the man Durnbaugh calls "the best manager I ever played for."

"He was down in Mobile," Durnbaugh explains, "and he said, 'Hey, I need you.' So I talked to my wife and she said, 'Go,' so I went down. If anybody else would've called I don't think I would've gone back, but I loved Ernie White. He would always try to help you and always talk the game with you. He was just an outstanding man."

Bobby Durnbaugh still watches baseball today.

"I like to go to minor league games here in Dayton," he says, "and watch these young kids make young kid's mistakes, and see how they position themselves, where they're playing and that type thing. I enjoy the game. I don't enjoy some of the antics some of them go through now, but I'm old school. That's not me."

Besides being one of just 32 short-time major league shortstops since the end of World War II, Brian Ostrosser is a rare bird for another reason. He's Canadian.

"As a kid," he says, "that's all I ever wanted to do. I was more into baseball than I was into hockey. I wasn't drafted. I was just kind of plucked off the farm here in Stoney Creek and given an opportunity to try my luck in St Petersburg, Florida, in 1970."

Ostrosser credits his ascent to a strong work ethic.

"I think it was because I was a good listener," he says.

"I was coachable, and I did have that little bit of Canadian hockey blood in me that I ran hard and I tried hard, and I think as the seasons went on they were using me as an example to run the bases and slide into second base to rip second base out of the ground type of thing. That's kind of the way I played. It wasn't dirty but it was aggressive."

So how does a young man born 20 years before Canada sees its first major league team decide that he wants to be a baseball player?

"I don't know," Ostrosser says. "I lived right across the street from an old school grounds. It was an old red brick building, and my parents knew where I was every day because I was throwing a ball against the wall hour after hour after hour, and fielding the ground ball as it came back to me. And I would throw it as hard as I could against the wall, then try to field it in any way, shape or form. And in our backyard we had this black walnut tree, and when the walnuts would fall I would pick them up in a bushel basket, and I'd throw them up in the air and hit them with a baseball bat."

In 1958, when he was nine years old, Little League baseball came to Stoney Creek, Ontario.

"I was one year too young to play," he says. "But I wanted to play so badly I just got myself ready so that when I turned 10 I was ready. I always seemed to do well from the time I was 10 to when I was 19 years old when a birddog from the New York Mets invited me to a tryout camp and I ended up signing on the spot."

It was 1969, the year of the Amazin' Miracle Mets.

"The only guy that approached me," Ostrosser says, "was a fellow by the name of John Sartorial, and he organized a tryout camp in Hamilton, Ontario. And when I went there I thought they were going to run me through a few drills or whatever, because he brought up a scout from the States. I thought they were going to hit me some groundballs and maybe throw some batting practice and make me run the bases, and here it was that at least two teams showed up, thirty or forty kids or whatever, and we ended up having an intra-squad game."

Crestfallen might be a word to describe the young Mr. Ostrosser when he discovered he was not the only player invited to try out that day. But he was ready.

"In Stoney Creek," he says, "most people are steel-workers, factory workers and everything—hard working and hard playing—and I think that's one of the reasons that we succeeded so much. Our infield practice wasn't just tapping the groundball to you. They drilled it at you. And so many times when we had an infield practice we had already intimidated our opposition because our coach or field manager, he hit the ball hard and we turned the double plays and we were very snappy, very quick, and we ran windsprints after every practice. But we loved to do it.

"So the first thing [the scouts] did was make us run the 100-yard dash, and I'm not that fast anymore, but I blew everybody away, and that made me feel confident. Then during the intra-squad game I went 3 for 4 and didn't make any errors, and after it was said and done they only wanted to talk to me. They wanted to come to my house and talk to my mother and father and myself and ask me if I was interested in taking a shot at it. Of course I was going to an organization that had just won the World Series, but I didn't care. I just wanted the opportunity to play."

The Mets gave Ostrosser a thousand dollars and a plane ticket to Florida.

"I went to spring training in 1970. And I ended up going to Marion, Virginia, my first year, in the Appalachian League. In '71 I was back in Pompano Beach, Florida, for the entire season.

"'In '72 I made the Double A team in Memphis, Tennessee, in the Texas League, and that's where I had my big year. I ended up being the MVP for the team, and I had a decent batting average until probably the last month of the season I kind of fell off a little bit. I never missed any games. I played every game and near the end of the year they sent me up to Tidewater in Triple A for the last two weeks of the season, and I think we finished fourth. But they have a playoff up there, and they inserted me at shortstop, and we ended up winning the International League and headed to Hawaii for some sort of series or championship. So that was year they put me on the 40-man roster. After three years I finally got on the 40-man roster."

And yet the somewhat rapid success didn't go to his head. He knew he still had a lot to learn.

"Whitey Herzog was my mentor. He was the head of the Mets minor league player development when I was coming up, and he kind of took me under his wing. I know when I went to the instructional league the year before he said, 'Look, if you're going to be in the major leagues as a utility infielder, shortstop or whatever, you've got to learn how to bunt.' I remember him taking me to Al Lang Field to the batting cages, and buckets and buckets of balls I had to bunt, bunt, bunt. I wasn't the fastest guy by a long shot, but that next year I ended up leading the league in bunt base hits and sacrifice bunts. So once again it was hard work more than anything. And luck. As I said, I was coachable was the main thing. I listened and I worked hard. I wasn't better than anybody else."

In 1973, the year he would eventually make his appearance in the majors, and the year that the Mets would return to the World Series, Ostrosser began the season at Triple A Tidewater. But then the story becomes a bit more involved.

"In my first major league spring training," he says, "we were running wind sprints, and I had a pain in my stomach. I thought, Here I am getting a stitch in my stomach, but I can't give in because I'm on the 40-man roster and I want to prove myself. So I kept running and running and running. It ended up my appendix had burst, and I missed most of spring training. I was in the hospital. It was a pretty big operation. And I came out of that probably 15 to 20 pounds lighter than my playing weight, and so I stayed on for extended spring training to get into playing shape. Once again, being on the 40-man roster meant a hell of a lot more than being in the minor leagues because I had major league ballplayers coming in my hospital room. Yogi Berra visited me. And this is a Yogi-ism. I'm laying in the hospital bed and I've got tubes down my nose, and I don't know what the hell's going on, and Yogi looked at me and says, 'Don't get too encouraged.' He says, 'Don't get too encouraged. We'll work things out.'

"I did get to Tidewater and it was probably the end of April, or maybe even the first part of May. Then in August Bud Harrelson cracked a bone in his sternum, so that opened up a spot for me. He went on the 15-day disabled list, I think, and that's when they called me up.

"I was in Pawtucket, Rhode Island and my manager, Johnny Antonelli, called me on the phone. He said, 'They need you in New York tomorrow morning.' I know it was a Saturday. They had the plane ticket for me and I got there and got to the hotel and somebody took me to the ballpark for a doubleheader against the St. Louis Cardinals."

If that doesn't sound quite sudden enough, Ostrosser's first major league appearance, less than 24 hours after being called up, was in that second game against St. Louis.

"Nobody knew I was there. My wife knew, but I couldn't get a hold of my parents. They were at one of my cousin's weddings or some darn thing, so I ended up playing in a major league game and nobody that I cared about really knew it, other than my wife. Of course, she was back home in Tidewater.

"Once I got to Shea Stadium and walked into the

locker room, I ran into the clubhouse attendant and introduced myself. He says, 'Here's your locker over in the corner.' And it had my uniform hanging in it. Willie Mays had a double locker, and I got his other half. It was full of his fan mail, so I put my glove and my spikes on top of all the fan mail. He had so much fan mail that he needed two lockers, but I got to use it for a little while. I just couldn't believe I was there."

Ostrosser struck out twice in his very first game.

"The ball looked as big as a basketball," he says. "I could not believe how easy it was to see the ball. I wish I could relive that moment, because I was looking at the right field fence every time I swung the bat. It just looked so nice coming in. It was Rick Wise, and all he threw me was fastballs, knee-high, right in my kitchen. It was something I should've been able to hit and I didn't. I think I fouled a couple off, but that was it. I struck out twice. I was pumped. I just didn't keep my eye on the ball."

Ostrosser managed to work his way into two games, one of them his only major league start, in San Francisco on a West Coast trip. Before his call-up he had never been to San Francisco. Or Los Angeles. Or San Diego. In fact, when he was called up by the Mets, he'd never even been to New York.

But in San Francisco, in the game Ostrosser didn't start, his Shea Stadium clubhouse neighbor, Willie Mays, pinch-hit for him. Mays doubled. It was Mays' last base hit at Candlestick Park. Soon the end would come for Brian Ostrosser as well. He managed one more game, as a late-inning replacement for Teddy Martinez, in San Diego. By the time the team returned home, Bud Harrelson was healthy enough to play.

"The day he came back I was headed to Tidewater." Ostrosser was left out of the September call-ups, most likely because teams in a pennant race often keep their rosters to a minimum to avoid distraction. He began the '74 season in Tidewater, but by June he had been traded to Oklahoma City, the Triple A farm team of the Cleveland Indians.

"I was kind of heartbroken," he says. "For whatever reason I wasn't playing well, and to this day I'll never be able to explain why. If I wasn't in a hitting slump I'd be in a fielding slump. I just couldn't get it going for whatever reason. So I went to Oklahoma City and turned it around a little bit."

But even that turnaround was short-lived. Trouble would raise its head again early in 1975.

"It was during the first week or two of the season, and we were in Indianapolis and Tom Hume threw me a nice slider low and in, and I drilled it right off my ankle and broke my ankle. That was the end. I ended up being on the disabled list for I don't know how long. I came back near the end of the year, and I couldn't run, but I was the designated hitter, played a little bit of first base, and had an operation in the off-season. They had to take a little piece of my hip and put it in the crack in my ankle, and I went to spring training in '76 and just couldn't run and they released me."

But Brian Ostrosser's story does have a happy end-

ing. He found work at the steel company that had
employed him during his baseball off-seasons and
stayed there for 30 years before retiring. He joined a
fast-pitch softball league and, not surprisingly, did quite
well. And the season following his retirement, the Indians moved their Triple A team to Toledo, just across the
border from Stoney Creek, Ontario.

"I had some good buddies in Toledo," he says, "so
my wife and I went down there many a weekend and I'd
take down a case of Labatt's Blue or Molson Canadian. I
think these guys enjoyed the good Canadian beer. The
Blue Jays were up and running at that time with guys
like Rick Cerone and Jim Norris, so I'd go down to
Toronto to see them play and we'd go for a beer or two
afterwards.

"You know, I did miss it. There's no ifs, ands, or buts
about it, but slowly but surely you get older and time
passes and everybody kind of fades into the sunset."

From the time Dennis Sherrill stepped onto a ballfield,
he was special. And everybody knew it. Like many men
who eventually play in the majors, whether they speak of
it or not, Dennis Sherrill was the best athlete on every
ballfield he ever played on. At least until he played pro-
fessionally.

"After I signed," Sherrill says, "I played in the Florida State League, which was skipping two leagues. I
moved up the ladder fast. Maybe too fast. Defensively I
could play. Offensively I was overmatched.

In 1974 Sherrill was the first round pick of the New

York Yankees, the twelfth pick overall. The first overall pick that year was shortstop Bill Almon, who went on to enjoy a 15-year major league career. The number three pick, Lonnie "Skates" Smith, played for 17 seasons. The number five pick, Dale Murphy, played on seven All-Star teams and won two MVP Awards. Garry Templeton was selected just after Sherrill. Four behind was Lance Parrish who, when he finally retired in 1995, had caught more major league games than all but six men in the history of baseball. Willie Wilson was taken at number 18, Rick Sutcliffe at number 21.

But those are numbers, and 18-year-old rookies are human beings. In Sherrill's first year as a pro the fastballs were faster. They had better movement. And the breaking pitches? Well, they broke even more.

"I went from hitting high school pitchers, from just owning high school pitchers, to facing Dennis Martinez. And he ate me up. I had no chance against a guy like that. Eventually you learn how to hit a little bit, but it takes awhile. You're very confident of your abilities, but after a while you're thinking, I'm trying as hard as I can try, and I'm just not able to do what I used to be able to do. It doesn't happen in one game. It's over a period of several games that you figure you have to make some adjustments. I'd never had to make any adjustments hardly, because I was just so much better than everybody else, and now you're up against guys that are as good as you, if not better."

But the Yankees had made an investment. Despite his frustration, despite his lack of success, Sherrill was moved up the minor league ladder. After a short season in the Florida State League he found himself in Double A.

"I only hit like a buck eighty, and probably a weak buck eighty," he says. "Then I moved up to the Eastern League and hit about .230, and that was kind of a weak .230. Defensively I made a lot of errors, a lot of senseless errors, young, inexperienced errors, but I showed that I had skills to make major league plays also. I moved up to Triple A the next year. I was the youngest guy in the league in Triple A.

"In hindsight, they moved me too fast, because I never really had a chance to build any confidence. I was pushed up the ladder because at that time the Yankees didn't have the strong team they have now, and shortstop was evidently a weakness."

Dennis Sherrill made two quick trips to the majors, once in 1978 and again in 1980. He made his Yankee debut on September 4th as a pinch-runner for Jim Spencer and came around to score on a Thurman Munson single in a 9-1 blowout of Detroit. It would be two years later, on June 22nd, before he started his first game and got his first and only major league base hit. It came against Oakland's Matt Keough, that season's American League Comeback Player of the Year.

Sherrill's last major league appearance came just six days later, on June 28th. Soon after he found himself back in Triple A. And at the end of the season he walked away from baseball.

"I'm sure glad I was able to play in the big leagues.

And I played two different years in the big leagues. That's a great thing. I'm very proud. Very, very proud."

But when you talk with Dennis Sherrill, you get the sense that what could have been, maybe even what was supposed to have been, outweighs what was. You get the sense that even though hindsight is supposedly 20/20, maybe the reflection of Sherrill's baseball career is still coming into focus.

"I don't put blame that I didn't play longer on anybody but myself," he says. "I walked away in 1980. That was my last year. And when I got out of baseball, that was my choice. I didn't get released. It wasn't fun anymore, and I really wanted to do something different in my life. It wasn't about money. I know that if I was going to become a rich man that would've been my best opportunity to do it. It was about me being happy. And from talking to a lot of other players, they felt the same way. You've got to remember that baseball players, that's all they know. From high school on, that was all I knew. Really, even before that. Maybe for someone looking at it on TV every day, they think it's this great job, but that's your whole life. Your whole life is baseball. I was a guy that had a lot of hobbies. I like to fish. I like to hunt. I like to do a lot of things, and baseball takes everything.

"The game was fun, but it's a business. And it gets kind of dirty. Just like every business anymore. I just wanted to play baseball. I could've gone to college, but when you're a first round pick there's pressure on you because the money's there and first round picks sign. They do. I wish the money then was what it is now, but it wasn't. So you do it. You go with that. And then you kind of put all your marbles in one basket, and being a first round pick makes it a little bit tougher to go to college after the season because they've got you playing in all these winter leagues. You have no time to do anything but play baseball. If it doesn't work for you, six or seven years down the road you're there with no experience in anything but baseball. So now you're trying to get a job and no one wants to hire you because you're part-time. What do you do? You're spending your bonus money to make ends meet and after a while it's like, This ain't cutting it anymore."

Sherrill says that his career highlight was being invited back to the Yankees' Old-Timer's Day in 2002. He took his son.

"He was born in 1980 and that was my last year. All he had ever heard were the stories, and now he got a chance to go up there and rub shoulders. He talked with Wade Boggs for quite a while. He sees me out there taking batting practice with Mattingly and Boggs and all these guys. That was the highlight of my baseball life, being able to share that with my son."

Maybe things look pretty good on reflection after all.

"You can define success in a lot of ways," Sherrill says. "And from a baseball standpoint they look at how great your numbers were and how many years you played and everything. Right now I've got two kids. My son's 25. My daughter's almost 22. I've got a great relationship with them, and I don't think I would have that if I would've stayed. To me that means more than any kind of career I would have ever had in baseball. And I'm still married to the same woman that I first married, so I'm doing just fine."

7TH

This is the End

Tell Me When it's Over

How do you know when it's over? When it's the right time? I'd always thought about that and I knew that I didn't want to be the guy hanging on, playing in the minor leagues, watching my skills deteriorate, just hanging on to be there. I just couldn't picture doing that, because I enjoyed playing so much and you play at such a high level that it was difficult to decide when that time would come.

I was released in mid-season. I came home, and I had calls from other teams to continue to play. I just thought 15 years was a long time. My kids were in school, and I was away from home a lot and I figured I'd had a great ride. I did everything I wanted to do, and it was the time to focus on my family and do the obligation that I had there. I knew I'd figure something out, but I hadn't really made any hard-and-fast plans. I was involved in a number of things, but I hadn't made a definite decision at that time. So I took the rest of that year off and basically did nothing except stuff with the family. We took a couple of vacations. We did the things that we wanted to do in the middle of the summer that we had never done. We had never really taken a summer vacation.

People always ask, Do you miss it? Well, obviously, I miss between the lines. I miss the game. I miss playing it, but it got to the point where I couldn't play the way I knew I should. You can really feel your skills deteriorate. You weren't doing things as well as you could do them in the past. And that's a tough realization, but I dealt with that. But the rest of it? No, you don't miss traveling three months of the year, living out of your suitcase, arriving at hotels at five in the morning and playing that night. You don't miss those parts. But the game itself? Yeah, you miss it. That was what you dreamed about. You got to live your dream.

— *Bill Almon*

In '72 I was playing in Japan, and I'd made their all-fielding shortstop. That's hard to do with those guys, because they're noted for their hands. But hitting-wise, the second year started off gangbusters. Me and Sadduharah Oh were the home run leaders the first two weeks. I knew they were going to be pitching me in after the first year, and I was ready for them. That plate seemed to widen up and everything started going away. I struggled after that. I could see that I wasn't going to get back in the big leagues, and the Dodgers had offered me an opportunity to manage a team. Tommy Lasorda put in a good word for me so I said, Well, let me

look at it from that side and see what I can do.
— *Bart Shirley*

The choice that I made was that I didn't hang around Atlanta when the Braves put me on waivers in '80. They put me on waivers and instead of me staying in Atlanta and waiting, just cool my heels there, I just packed up out of frustration and took my family back to South Texas. So those are decisions that I made that cost me from getting another four or five years in the big leagues.
— *Larvell Blanks*

I wanted to get a big league invite to a camp, and if I wouldn't have made a team I might've just called it quits. But at that point you owe it to yourself to at least try. I don't think my heart was into it over the winter. I ended up getting sent down to Omaha and finishing out my year there, but I actually did very well the last month there after I came off the DL. I think I was hitting .210 or something when they put me on the DL in July, and then I came back for the last month and did pretty well, almost doing it on fumes, almost just for myself, knowing it wasn't going to matter. At the end of that year I knew I was tired of it, I was done. I'd been through too much. It wasn't as fun anymore.
— *Paul Zuvella*

It was easy for me because I had a very bad ankle my final year. I couldn't play. It was the only time I was not the starting shortstop. I started the first six games for the Phillies and ended up in the hospital with cellulitis, and they didn't give me enough antibiotics and the infection settled deep in my ankle joint, and if I played I couldn't walk for two days after that. It was torture. There's nothing worse, if you've been a regular all your life, than not being able to play period. It was very easy to retire.

— *Dick Groat*

Looking Back

If I could've learned how to hit earlier in my career I probably would've got 2,700 or 2,800 hits. I got 2,200, right around 2,200, and I was considered an out my first three or four years. I didn't start switch-hitting until my first year of Triple A. If I could've done it all over again, and my dad even said that before he passed away. God, he said, if we could've started switch-hitting earlier it would've been a lot better.

But I really did everything I wanted to. I played in All-Star games, I got Gold Gloves, I hit .300, I won the World Series, I led the league in fielding. I can't say I cheated myself out of anything. I worked for everything. I never shortcut myself or my teammates. I was an over-achiever, because there were a lot of guys that had more ability than I did. If I didn't overachieve I would've never made it to the big leagues. I look at guys with great ability, even now, and they do things so effortlessly. I knew I had to work harder than Joe Schmoe because he was better than I was. And I'm glad I was raised that way.

I'm glad I had to play hungry every year. I started making All-Star teams in '75, but even after five or six years in the big leagues as a bonafide shortstop, I went to spring training every year with the attitude that I had to try to win a job. I think that's what motivated me. My dad said, Never take anything for granted. You've got to win your job every year, no matter what you did the year before, and I think that was a big influence in my life.

— *Larry Bowa*

The best opportunity that I had as a shortstop was probably in 1979 with Texas when we finished a half game behind either California or Kansas City to get in the playoffs. We lost eleven out of the first twelve ballgames. Had I have played shortstop that season, I can almost guarantee that we would've made the playoffs. I was 29 years old. Not quite in my prime but ready to play. I got to spring training two weeks before everybody. Worked like a dog thinking I was going to get a chance to play. You know, stick him in there. Let him play 50 games in a row and see what he does. But no. I sat on the bench from Day One. I'd go in there, drive in two runs, score two runs, and make a bobble at short, the next day I was out. And Texas has never won anything. In '79, that was the time for them to do it if I'd have played short. That's my opinion.

— *Larvell Blanks*

Bill Virdon tabbed me as the shortstop for the next 10 years, and I don't know if that was the right thing to do.

I was a frail 6'1" 165 pounds and a guy that was touted. Houston didn't have much in their farm system, and I was traded from the Yankees. They had a lot of short-stops. In Houston they tried to make me a switch-hitter at Triple A. I went to the big leagues hitting left-handed. I remember getting a double off Tom Hume with Cincinnati, left-handed, at the big league level. And I only had a half season, or maybe three-quarters of a season, switch-hitting, and at that point I was only 21 years old when I first got called up. I wish I would've switch-hit but started earlier in my career. So I ended up going to winter ball, and at that point I wanted to stay in the big leagues so I gave up switch-hitting so I could try to make teams. I didn't want to be the guy that was the switch-hitter and had to go back for more seasoning. I wanted to stay at the major league level.

— *Mike Fischlin*

The way I look at it is everybody's career is an unfinished book, and very rare is the athlete anywhere that has the complete book. If they tell you they do, I don't know if they're totally being honest. Even the superstars wish for something more or something else or something different. Maybe it's that one World Series ring or that opportunity to win the Triple Crown. Whatever it was, everybody's career is an unfinished book.

— *Paul Zuvella*

I regret that I didn't have the opportunity to play at least both sports for two or three years, but Mr. Rickey

would not buy it, and I'm not sure that Mr. Rickey wasn't right, because I was a bonus player.
— *Dick Groat*

What it Takes
Quick feet first. Good hands. A strong arm. The way guys are built right now, obviously you want a guy that's tall and not skinny but lean. Nomar. Jeter. Tejada. A-Rod's a little bit bigger. Furcal's a little bit smaller but he's a very good shortstop.
— *Larry Bowa*

Good range, good arm, nice soft hands. The shortstop's definitely referred to as the captain of the infield. He's in the middle of the mix. He gets the majority of the plays. He's a guy you can depend on to make that out.
— *Desi Relaford*

Good hands. You can't have someone with iron hands on the infield. Then you've got to have a certain amount of speed and quickness. And the arm. I don't think size is important at shortstop. Your arm is important, and your hands are important. And you have to move your feet. What difference does it make if you're 5'4" and you can get to everything and throw people out? You don't have to be 6'1" or 6'3" to play shortstop. Because you're not really expected to hit the home runs and stuff like that. You're supposed to just be a sound defensive player
— *Jack Kubiszyn*

Every fielding play you make has to be clean. If it's not clean, you miss the guy. At second base you can fumble it and get the guy. Third base, you can do the same thing. If the ball's hit kind of firm, and it bounces you can pick it up. But you ain't going to do that at shortstop.
— *Alex Grammas*

Shortstop was really my natural position. I had a good arm and I had a good, quick release, and I was as good as anybody in the organization at that. Shortstop, to me, that's the position where most of the ground balls are hit, and you've got to be involved on just about every play, and you've got to be thinking. I think the key to playing shortstop is anticipation.
— *Bart Shirley*

You have to have a lot of range playing shortstop, obviously moreso than third. Second basemen range a lot, but it's a little different at second because you're so close to first you've got more time on ground balls than you do at shortstop. At shortstop you have to field it cleanly, you have to make a good throw. Period. At second you can bobble one and still make the out, but I think short is more demanding because of the range. I liked second because it was a little bit of relief. Third and short were more demanding, because you had to make the perfect throw. Second wasn't as, I don't know, intense maybe.
— *Bill Spiers*

It's a skill position. You've got to catch the ball clean. You've got to have some range. And then you have to have a really strong arm.

— *Larvell Blanks*

You need the complete set of tools. You've got to have the speed, the range. You've definitely got to have the ability to field ground balls. You've got to have the strongest arm because there is no room for error. You've got to be very athletic because turning the plays around second base requires very agile movement. The thing that is nice about baseball and shortstops is it really is not a position where size is a big factor. I mean, it's nice to be like Alex Rodriguez and that size, but you can be Ozzie Smith's size and still be tremendously successful on the defensive side. Size, to me, is not a factor. [David] Eckstein is a perfect example.

— *Bill Almon*

You have to be lucky to get there. You have to be at the right place at the right time. And a lot of people aren't. There are a lot of good shortstops that don't make it.

— *Don Buddin*

A Bit of Advice
You've got to keep your head down on ground balls. And every time you're out there, just say, Hit me the ball, hit me the ball. And always be ready. When a batter came up I knew who was running. I knew that if the ball went this way what would I do. It's just like a computer

went through my head and I had all the angles figured out, what I was going to do before the ball was hit. I don't know if everybody does that, but I just wanted to make sure I covered every angle on every hitter.

— *Daryl Spencer*

You've got to keep your focus and stay down on the ball. Keep your butt down and so forth. You've got to learn to go to your right and your left and come in on the ball. And throw accurately. You don't have to have a terrific arm. You've got to remember who's running. If Yogi Berra's running, you don't have to throw as hard to first base.

— *Don Buddin*

The best thing to teach players is to keep your feet moving. You can't get on your heels. Once you get on your heels, you're dead at shortstop. You've got to keep your feet moving, and once you get your feet moving they get in the right place to field the ball.

— *Mike Fischlin*

The Glove
Some guys can't use a glove until it's totally broken in, and then they've got to keep it until it just about falls off their hand. Then you get some guys that take it out of the box, use it one or two days in batting practice, and then they start using it in games. And how they break them in, it's all over the spectrum. You listen to guys and you have some of your own thoughts. When I was play-

ing shortstop every day, I would go through at least two gloves a year, game-type gloves. I would have a game glove for Opening Day which was usually the ending glove for last year, but during all of spring training I was working on a new one that would be coming into play relatively quickly. And I would have one right behind that so when Opening Day started that would be my batting practice glove, so there was always three in the mix. I always used the Wilson 2000. I liked the glove. I thought it gave me at least the flexibility with the size. It was small enough yet big enough, and I always liked the leather that they had.

— *Bill Almon*

I kept a glove an entire season, then I broke another one in the next spring. I used Rawlings gloves all my life.

— *Dick Groat*

The Best I've Ever Seen
Because of his agility, being able to leave your feet and get up without skipping a beat, I'd have to say Ozzie. And Vizquel's real close. I'd have to say those two guys. Belanger was very good in his day.

— *Larry Bowa*

When we were playing it was Roy McMillan of Cincinnati. He was the best defensively. He reminded me of Vizquel, the guy that's the best with the glove now. He could round up the ball. He was always in position.

— *Eddie O'Brien*

MARK BELANGER

Transcendental Graphics

Probably Luis Aparicio. We played against him when I was with the Angels. He was with Chicago then. He's a lot like Vizquel, but I think he had a little more range and a better arm than Vizquel.

— *Joe Koppe*

He was probably at the end of his career, but Dal Maxvill when I first came up was just incredible. I never saw him catch a ball. Like, it didn't matter if the ball was in the hole, it just deflected from his glove. He never caught a ball. And I can only imagine what he was like in his prime. But here's a guy who didn't have an incredible arm, but he knew how to play hitters. He knew how to rid of the ball. He could turn the double play. You look at him and it was just grace. He'd catch a ball in the hole sometimes and flip it underhand, and it would just get there. You'd look at him and go, How did he do that? There's guys like Cal Ripken and Dal Maxvill that make their careers longer because they know there's more than just catching and throwing the ball. They study hitters, they study their pitching staff, and they know situations and what the hitter can do in this situation. You think you've got a base hit and the next thing you look up and he's got the ball.

— *Roger Metzger*

The first guy that comes to my mind is Davey Concepcion, because I played with him in Venezuela, and I know he played on AstroTurf all those years. But I remember playing a game with Davey down in

Venezuela, and the first ball hit, I was playing second and I came in to get a double play with him and the ball went right between his legs. I mean, routine grounder. And he kind of looked at me, you know, so we had runners on first and second and another ball hit, routine, and it went right between his legs again. And I was shocked. Here's this major league hero of mine, and he just looked at me and he goes, Bobby, I'm only human.

— *Bobby Bonner*

DAVE CONCEPCION

I caught Roy McMillan at the tail end of his playing days, and they say in his prime he was so consistent. He just knew how to make the plays. He was always in front of the ball it seemed like. Here's a guy that wore glasses. You'd think that would take away from him, but not him. He was making the plays every day. I didn't see him doing a whole lot of backhand stuff, but he was always rounding that ball off and getting in front of it and making the plays, just being so consistent.

— *Bart Shirley*

Ozzie Smith was fantastic, but the guy I like to watch most is Omar Vizquel. I'd like to have a film clip of when he and Alomar were at Cleveland, some of their outstanding plays, because those two guys were really fantastic around second base. You can't tell about a player unless you play right next to him, but from what I've seen on TV I don't know anybody that can be better than Vizquel.

— *Daryl Spencer*

I guess when I played Aparicio was as good as there was. He had good range, he had a good arm, and he could run like the devil. And he made all the plays. He didn't back away from any ground balls. He went after everything.

— *Don Buddin*

The most exciting player had to have been Maury Wills for the simple fact he was good defense, he had speed, and when I was watching him as a kid that's when he was doing all the base stealing and setting the records, so offensively, defensively he was exciting.

— *Bruce Christensen*

Defensively the best shortstop I ever saw was Ozzie. When he was with the Padres he was probably good, but he wasn't polished yet. He didn't yet understand all the intricacies of the position and the game at that point. He was that good. You could see it. But then when he went to the Cardinals he started to mature. At that point he understood the whole game. He understood the

Brian Bahr / AFP / Getty Images

OZZIE SMITH

The SHORTSTOP

pitchers, the pitches. He understood everything about
it. He was complete. He became like a Ripken in the
knowledge, but unlike Cal he was able to put together
that range and that acrobatic ability that nobody ever
seemed to be able to match.

— *Bill Almon*

I saw Marty Marion when I was a kid. He was magnifi-
cent. I guess during the years that I played, Roy McMillan was as good as there was. They had marvelous
hands. They always got in front of the ball. They both
had good arms, very accurate arms, great release, and
excellent feet. And excellent instincts.

— *Dick Groat*

Baseball Today

They're better batters right now, there's no question
about it. Don't ask me. I don't know why. I watch them
on TV and think, I could never make that play. I made
some good plays. Some great plays. But not the way they
do it today. They've got great hands, and outstanding
body control. I couldn't dive and catch balls the way
they do. I just couldn't. But this bare-handed stuff that
you see today—as long as the ball's rolling you put your
glove on it. I get a kick out of them thinking you can get
rid of the ball quicker if you take it bare-handed. You
can't. If you get it with a glove you've still got to come
back with your arm to throw, and if you catch with your
bare hand you're going to still have to come back to
throw. The secret of coming in on slow-hit balls is to

170

MARTY MARION

Hulton Archive/Getty Images

time it so that as you catch it, when that right foot hits, you're throwing. Otherwise you take two steps to throw. And that's the secret of fielding slow-hit balls. Not the fact that you try to catch it with your bare hand. I get irritated when I see it on TV, because so many balls are missed because of that. Occasionally a guy will make one and everybody will give him a hand and think it's a great play. To me it's not a great play. It's not great at all.

— *Alex Grammas*

We were always taught to curl up and get our bodies going to where we need to throw, get your weight going towards first base. And I was very good at the curl hop. I think that gives you a good, accurate, strong approach to making sure you're almost knocking the first baseman over. Because you've got weight going that way, you've got your arm going that way. The biggest thing I see at short, second, third, whatever, is lazy feet. They all kind of stop and then just flip it over there. They don't use their feet to throw. That may be because they have stronger arms and they don't have to, but I think it can be a way to make more errors because you're being lazy. If you use your feet all the time, you make more accurate throws more of the time.

— *Mike Fischlin*

I can't stand to watch. I like to watch kids because kids give you everything. Now things have changed so much. They're so overpaid it's absurd. I would've paid them to play, because it's always fun. When things aren't fun,

you should get out of it. Life's too dang short.
— *Jack Kubiszyn*

I tell people it's a good thing I played when I did. They say, "Don't you wish you could play today because you could make ten, twelve million dollars." And I say, "I'm glad I don't because I'm looking at some of these guys." But you know, everything's relative. You've got to think back to the training techniques that were in place in the 50s, 60s and 70s. Today, starting about the late 70s and really getting hot and heavy in the 80s was weight training. I'm not saying I could be as bulky as Tejada, but I think given the opportunities to train the way the younger kids today train there's probably a possibility. In baseball when I was a kid, and going through high school and even college, you better not get caught in the weight room. Today it's modified weight training and high school kids, in the off-season, are going through weight training. I worked out with free weights, but we didn't have a Nautilus machine. We didn't have all the training facilities they do now. The focus was on just playing the raw game. That's how you get better.
— *Roger Metzger*

The guys miss cutoffs. The winning run could be on first base and he goes to steal second and the catcher makes a bad throw. We used to get in front of the ball and let it hit us some place. They let it go into center field and the winning run goes to third. I don't think they understand situations. The athletes are better of course, and my God

Transcendental Graphics

FREDDIE PATEK

the shortstops just went to a new level the way they play. The hitters are stronger, but I think the ball's juiced up a little bit, and the ballparks are a little smaller.

— *Daryl Spencer*

I watch baseball now. It's the same game. I can sit in the stands and know when a hitter has to move a runner over. I can see the fundamental mistakes that they make running bases, and I know exactly what happened, why it happened. I can see the pitcher's mistakes. Watching major league baseball players at a baseball game, it's real exciting for me. Those guys do some amazing things.

— *Larvell Blanks*

I got my kids into Little League and tee ball and the whole thing. I wanted them to be fans also. I had grown up a Red Sox fan so that's what they are. We're lucky here. We're only a short jaunt up to Pawtucket where we catch the Triple A. High quality and good ball, and you see a lot of good players. So we're able to continue that because I didn't lose my love for the game. I just needed six months away from it. We go there and we still run out to Fenway. It's a little bit more of a jaunt. But it's so tough to get tickets. On my pass I can walk in, but most places will give you tickets to sit down. At Fenway they don't. They just give you standing-room-only because they don't have tickets. We follow the Red Sox closely, but I follow baseball. If the Red Sox aren't on I'll turn on the Braves, ESPN, so if the TV's on in my house

there's usually a game on it. And that goes for the whole family. They'll always turn on a game.
— *Bill Almon*

It's just diluted to the point where it's embarrassing. A couple of my friends that broadcast major league baseball always laugh when they tell me, "Dick, you don't have any idea." It's the way the game is played that bothers me more than anything. One of the things I've always loved about basketball, it's the epitome of a team game. You have to be unselfish. You can't run a lick as a football player if you don't have somebody to block up front. Baseball is just as much of a team game, but it's no longer played as a team game because the agents won't let them be team players. Go for yourself and make your money and make my money.

I watch a team with some good-looking youngsters here in Pittsburgh right now, but they don't have the vaguest idea how to produce a run. Hit a double and hit a single. That's how you score. Hit a single and hit a home run. They don't advance runners because they don't play the game the way we were taught. It's a combination of things, and it's kind of disappointing because you have guys that really should be learning how to play the game in the minor leagues that are already in the major leagues and not able to handle it.
— *Dick Groat*

They don't know what fundamentals are anymore.
— *Don Buddin*

8TH

The Chapter in Which We Expound on the Significance of Cal Ripken Jr.

While Honus Wagner and Ozzie Smith, respectively, are the greatest offensive and defensive short-stops to ever play the game, no man has so greatly affect-ed the position in our life and times as Cal Ripken Jr. Ripken was the 1982 American League Rookie of the Year, a 19-time American League All-Star, a two-time All-Star Game MVP, a two-time Gold Glove winner, and a two-time MVP.

There's also a little thing called The Streak, a near unfathomable effort of everydayness unequalled in major league annals. But that's just the beginning. Well, maybe not the beginning, because actually none of that explains why Cal Ripken Jr. is the most pivotal shortstop of all time.

Bobby Bonner, the man anointed to receive the proverbial torch from longtime Oriole middle infielder Mark Belanger, might disagree. Don't get me wrong. Bobby Bonner admires Cal Ripken Jr. as much as any man can admire another man who pretty much took his job away from him.

Stuart Cahill/AFP/Getty Images

CAL RIPKEN JR.

"As a matter of fact," Bobby Bonner says, "I believe Ripken saved baseball."

A case can certainly be made that Ripken Jr., specifically in the aftermath of 1981 strike, made a shoestring grab of the pastime's popularity. Cal Ripken Jr., in many ways, looms larger than the position he played. He's wholesome as the dickens, the personification of the Protestant work ethic. Following the 1981 baseball strike, Ripken was a fresh face of freshness, a boy king poised to lead the masses out of their disillusionment and one of the few positives in a professional sport seemingly overwhelmed by self-interest. Because Cal, you see, just wanted to play.

Of course, many fans will tell you that, in his final years, Ripken and his run of consecutive appearances overwhelmed not only his position but his own Baltimore Orioles. It's certainly possible that not only Cal, but various and sundry managers, front office personnel, and even the Orioles organization as a whole were, at one time or another, held prisoner by The Streak.

But I contend that Ripken changed the way we view the position of shortstop for reasons other than the multiple awards, reasons other than The Streak (as consciousness grabbing as it was). Without Cal Ripken Jr., Derek Jeter, Yankee captain, two-time Gold Glove winner and owner of four World Championship rings, isn't a shortstop. Without Cal Ripken Jr., Alex Rodriguez, the American League MVP two of the last three years and the highest-paid player in the game, isn't a shortstop (and I know what you're saying, but on any other team outside of The Bronx and maybe Baltimore Alex Rodriguez, a two-time Gold Glove winner at the position, is a shortstop).

Yea, verily I say unto you that Cal Ripken Jr. changed the way we view the position of shortstop because he was a big old boy who not only found a home but succeeded mightily in a place where big old boys weren't exactly welcome. Old school baseball types have, since time immemorial, espoused that teams had to be strong up the middle. And by strong, those old schoolers didn't mean physically strong. In fact, just the opposite is more likely true. Strong up the middle means that you want top notch defensive players straight through the core of the diamond—a first-rate pitcher on the mound, a wily and protective catcher behind the plate, a speedy centerfielder to patrol the field's largest environs, and the best double-play combination possible to anchor the middle infield.

Your power belongs on the corners—first and third, left field and right. That's where you keep your offense stored away like a family secret, brought to light only in the offensive half of the inning.

It stands to reason that in order for a center fielder to cover a lot of ground he's got to be quick, fast. He's got to have a propensity for mobility. He must possess range.

Same goes for your middle infield. Especially shortstop. The shortstop is responsible for more infield acreage than any of his teammates, so you want someone with ease of movement, lots of range, a human joystick as it were. And, as the story logically goes, smaller men move better than bigger men. Which is why nearly every damn major league shortstop who once upon a time grabbed a starting position and held onto it until they all lived happily after was not the guy posting up in the paint during his team's off-season basketball games. In the good old days, major league shortstops came equipped with names like Rabbit (Walter James Vincent Maranville), Scooter (Philip Francis Rizzuto) and Pee Wee (Harold Henry Reese).

That is until the Iron Man (Calvin Edward Ripken Jr.) came along.

But let's back up for a second, back to the aforementioned beginning. Because no duly licensed baseball writer (not that I'm duly licensed to do much of anything outside of operating a motor vehicle within New York State; I'm just saying) worth his salt can spew forth an entire chapter on the significance of Cal Ripken Jr. without discussing The Streak. Because out there among us, there are some verifiable (and possibly duly licensed) Streak Freaks. So here, without further ado, is the genesis:

In the beginning, Cal Ripken Jr. was born on August 4, 1960, the second of four children, to Violet and Cal Ripken Sr. At the time, Cal Sr., a future major league coach and manager for the Baltimore Orioles, toiled as a minor league catcher. Baseball, you see, courses through the Ripken family blood.

In 1978, Ripken Jr., through nary a drop of nepotism, was selected by Baltimore in the second round of the amateur draft. He signed his contract immediately and after two full seasons in the minors made his major league debut on August 10, 1981, as a pinch-runner for Ken Singleton.

The Orioles, playing at home, were tied with the Kansas City Royals in the bottom of the twelfth when Ripken came around to score the winning run on a base hit by John Lowenstein. Two days later, in the second game of a doubleheader against those same Royals, Ripken would get his first major league start. At third base.

But this story decidedly picks up steam the following season, on July 1, 1982, when Ripken. entered Baltimore's lineup at shortstop, the position he would play until July 15, 1996. Fourteen years. Every day. Makes you kind of tired just thinking about it.

During Ripken's run from July to July, 1982 to 1996, over 300 other shortstops would start major league games and, before it was over, Ripken's consecutive games at short would total 2,216, a major league record at any position.

The Streak, however, actually began over a month earlier, on May 30, 1982, with Ripken still at third. And his consecutive game run would eclipse Lou Gehrig's on September 7, 1995, and not come to an end until September 20, 1998, after a remarkable stretch of 2,632 games.

How did this come to pass? I'm glad you asked.

In 1997, while The Streak was ongoing, Ripken published his autobiography, *The Only Way I Know*. One of the readily apparent themes is Ripken's belief that he was in the right place at the right time. This is obviously an extremely modest take on a Hall of Fame career, and yet more than a grain of truth percolates.

From 1968 to 1981, one of the best defensive short-stops in baseball history, Mark Belanger (he won eight Gold Gloves, including six in a row), held down the position for Baltimore. Belanger succeeded Hall of Famer Luis Aparicio. During Belanger's tenure the Ori-oles won six division titles, three American League pennants and one World Series.

But, for Baltimore, as well as for the rest of the country, 1981, Belanger's final season in an Oriole uniform, was a transition year. It was a time of impending excess. A time when bigger was better and aspirations of mo' better rushed aplenty. A time when Americans looked in the mirror, took a deep breath and said, I not only want my air, I want your air. I want all the air. Give me all the air. Now. Gimme gimme gimme. In 1981 the average salary for a major league ballplayer was $196,500, less than two-thirds today's minimum salary but exponentially higher than it had been just a decade before. And this expansion, this lust, this symbolic land grab wasn't just within the business of baseball. Absolutely not.

On Opening Day 1981, Fleetwood Mac's *Tusk*, the follow-up to the most successful single album in record-ed music history (*Rumours*), as well as the most expensive album ever produced at the time of its release, was less than two years old.

On Opening Day 1981, director Michael Cimino's

Heaven's Gate, the follow-up to the his Oscar-winning film *The Deer Hunter*, as well as the most expensive film ever made, was less than six months into its theatrical release. Ronald Reagan, whose presidency would usher in a decade of record profits on Wall Street (the Dow Jones Average would more than double during his eight years as President) and inspire Oliver Stone's eponymous movie (which in turn cemented "greed is good" as a national catch phrase), had been in office less than three months.

That year also marked not only Cal Ripken Jr.'s major league debut, but baseball's longest strike to date. The players walked mid-season and only 105 games were played. For the first time in major league history, teams were awarded playoff spots based on half-season finishes. The strike, like most, was ugly. Big-time ugly. In fact, if the strike had been a long division problem, the remainder would be hard feelings. Mark Belanger was Baltimore's player representative in 1981, and in 1982 he was no longer with the club. For the first time in his professional career, which began when he signed with Baltimore in 1962, Belanger was no longer an Oriole.

Doug DeCinces, the club's starting third baseman since 1979 and a Baltimore draft pick in 1970, served as the American League's player rep during the '81 strike, and he, like Belanger, also found himself in a new uniform for the start of the '82 season (what did I tell you about the remainder of hard feelings?). Without Earl Weaver's approval, Baltimore's front office traded DeCinces to the California Angels, ostensibly opening up a spot at third for the young Ripken. But the often contrary, often contradictory, often contumacious Earl Weaver had other ideas. Somewhere in the English-speaking world there likely exists a dictionary with Earl Weaver's picture beside the entry for "colorful." Weaver was ejected from more ballgames (91) than any other manager in major league history. He never played in the major leagues, yet reached the Hall of Fame as a manager. And Weaver ran his Baltimore clubs with an abundance of spirit, a resolute will and an unshakable faith in good pitching supported by the three-run homer. Long before the world had heard of Oliver Stone, Earl Weaver could testify that greed is good.

Earl Weaver grew up in St. Louis, Missouri. When Weaver was fourteen years old, 6'2", 170 pound St. Louis Browns (the organization from which the Orioles were born) shortstop Marty Marion, the one and only "big" shortstop of his generation, won the American League MVP Award. Later Marion would manage the Browns, a position he would relinquish when the franchise moved to Baltimore.

In Mark Belanger's seventeen seasons with the Orioles he delivered but 20 home runs. You could count the number of round trippers in Belanger's most power productive season, 1974, on one hand. Even Belanger's batting average, a career .228, was miniscule.

Is it any wonder that Earl Weaver wanted more?

According to legend, the young Ripken reminded his manager of Marty Marion, a big shortstop with soft hands. But at the beginning of the 1982 season, with

both Belanger and DeCinces exiled to California, Weaver, as the Baltimore front office wanted, rotated Lenn Sakata and Bobby Bonner, Belanger's assumed replacement, at short. Bonner and Ripken had played together at Triple A Rochester. They were, in fact, side by side in the infield—Bonner at short and Ripken at third—for the longest game in professional baseball history, a 33-inning loss to Pawtucket (another likely Hall of Famer, Wade Boggs, played third that night for the PawSox).

On Ripken's 1982 Topps rookie baseball card (suggested retail price: $50), he and Bonner are together again, side by side. Bonner is listed as the shortstop, Ripken as the third baseman. So when the 1982 season began, Cal Ripken Jr. was the Orioles' starting third baseman (he went three for five with a homer and two RBI). Sakata, at 5'9" 160, appeared in 136 total games and hit six home runs. Bonner, at 6'0" 185 pounds, played in just 41 games and tallied none. By contrast, Ripken, now standing 6'4" and working his way up to 225 pounds, played 160 games and hit 28 home runs.

But in the eyes of many (including nearly every old schooled baseball mind), Ripken was too big, much too big, to play shortstop. Why? Because, save for Marty Marion, every successful major league shortstop to precede him was smaller. By the proverbial wide margin. Of the nineteen men inducted into the Baseball Hall of Fame at shortstop, Ripken stands four inches taller than the tallest (Robin Yount at 6'0") and twenty-five pounds heavier than the heaviest (Honus Wagner at 200). Rip-

Transcendental Graphics

RABBIT MARANVILLE

ken is seven inches taller than the Hall of Fame mean of 5'9" and ten inches taller than Rabbit Maranville and Phil Rizzuto.

Of course in recent times all sports have seen an increase in the size of their athletes, but Ripken, by comparison, even towers over the standout shortstops a mere generation before. In fact, when Ripken began his rookie season, only four former Gold Glove winners at short—Belanger, Jim Fregosi, Bobby Wine and Dave Concepcion (all 6'1")—were taller than six feet. And none came close to matching Ripken's weight.

The suggestion that Ripken was "too big" to play shortstop was, of course, a backhanded way of suggesting that he didn't possess the necessary mobility for the position. Just ten days after Ripken's first start at short, no less than future ESPN analyst Peter Gammons wrote for the Boston Globe, "Earl Weaver weakened two positions in his infield last week by moving rookie Cal Ripken Jr. to short and putting Honey Bear Rayford at third."

What Gammons was questioning, of course, was Ripken's range.

Yet now, thanks to the miracle of modern science and baseball statisticians across America, a fielder's range can be measured. We call it the Range Factor. A player's Range Factor is derived by adding his Assists and Put Outs, then dividing by the number of Games Played. Like bowling, a higher number is better in that it suggests that a player is able to reach more balls.

But there are obvious flaws.

A shortstop playing behind the Diamondbacks'
Brandon Webb, a sinkerball pitcher of the first degree,
or further back, Mark "The Bird" Fidrych, will have a
higher Range Factor than a shortstop supporting practi-
tioners of the high fastball, say Roger Clemens or Nolan
Ryan. A shortstop playing behind a left-handed pitcher
should have a higher Range Factor than a shortstop
playing behind a right-hander, because a left-hander
will face more right-handed batters who are more likely
to pull the ball, therefore giving the shortstop more
chances to make a play.

If Jason Giambi or Ted Williams, notorious left-
handed pull hitters, took all nine spots in the batting
order, a shortstop's Range Factor for those games would
be close to zero. So like the shift utilized against both
Giambi and Williams, the Range Factor system does possess its own gaping holes.

Defensively, however, Ripken held up fairly well his
first season (if he hadn't, of course, this would be an
entirely different chapter), making just 13 errors in 94
games at his new position. In 1982 Ripken got to half a
ball per game more than the average American League
shortstop. Nevertheless, Ripken's manager continued
to be questioned, particularly after a 19-game slump
that saw the rookie shortstop bat less than .150. A
month following his "weakened two positions" com-
ment, Gammons had Weaver on the defensive again.

"First," Weaver said of Ripken, "I think he's the best
defensive shortstop in our organization. And, second, I
think it will be easier down the line for the club to find

offense at third than it is at short."

Weaver's second argument becomes primary here. It's likely that his first retort is a justification, a rationalization, a little (or medium-sized) white lie. While his theory of more readily available third base power is true, the manager retired without finding consistent offensive production at the corner of his own squad. Bobby Bonner, by nearly all accounts, was the best defensive shortstop in the Orioles' organization in 1982, but a single play two years earlier, recounted similarly by both Ripken in his autobiography and Bonner, turned the impetuous Weaver against him and paved the way for Ripken's move to short.

Bonner, Ripken writes, was "Belanger's heir apparent . . . When we were on the same field in Bluefield, he made me look like a klutz."

But a miscue in Bonner's first major league appearance cost Baltimore the ballgame.

"I made an error in Toronto in 1980 on a wet field," Bonner says. "It had been raining, and Barry Bonnell hit a shot to my right. I never even got a glove on it. It went right through before I could even breathe, and Earl cussed me out because I didn't catch the ball."

"My father," Ripken writes, "said it was practically an impossible chance, but Earl didn't see it that way. The scene in the clubhouse afterward wasn't nice."

Though Bonner did play more games for Baltimore, his shot to become the Orioles' next shortstop, their next Mark Belanger, pretty much evaporated in the Toronto mist. So Barry Bonnell's sharply hit, extra-inning grounder gave Earl Weaver an excuse to look for a new shortstop. And while he was perusing, Weaver decided to grab 20 home runs a season, maybe 30, out of the position instead of the pedestrian 5 or 10. And Cal Ripken Jr., to his great credit, took advantage of the opportunity.

Though he did not fit the stereotypical shortstop mold, Ripken was a coach's son and a student of the game. What he lacked in physical quickness he made up for with instinct and intellect. Ripken's study of opposing hitters yielded what many saw as an almost surreal aptitude for positioning himself in just the right place, as if he knew where the ball would travel before it was even hit. In fact, despite his relatively abundant size and comparable lack of mobility, Cal Ripken Jr. maintained a range factor above the league average—well above the league average—for most of his early years as a shortstop.

In 1983 he improved to .7 of a ball above the league average. In 1984 a whopping ball and a half above the league average. The gap narrowed in 1990, again in 1992, until 1994, after a dozen years of daily play at baseball's second most physically demanding position when Ripken's range factor actually fell below the American League average. Not every battle can be won through hard work and intellect and instinct.

In 1997, at the age of 36 and following 2306 games at shortstop, Cal Ripken Jr. moved back to third base. But by then he had not only opened the door for men of size and power, but knocked the sucker flat.

9TH

The Lists

MVP Shortstops

1925	AL	Roger Peckinpaugh
1944	NL	Marty Marion
1948	AL	Lou Boudreau
1950	AL	Phil Rizzuto
1958	NL	Ernie Banks
1959	NL	Ernie Banks
1960	NL	Dick Groat
1965	AL	Zoilo Versalles
1982	AL	Robin Yount
1983	AL	Cal Ripken Jr.
1995	NL	Barry Larkin
2002	AL	Miguel Tejada
2003	AL	Alex Rodriguez

MLB

MIGUEL TEJADA

Gold Glove Shortstops

YEAR	SS	TEAM
1957 ML	Roy McMillan	Cincinnati Redlegs
1958 NL	Roy McMillan	Cincinnati Redlegs
1958 AL	Luis Aparicio	Chicago White Sox
1959 NL	Roy McMillan	Cincinnati Redlegs
1959 AL	Luis Aparicio	Chicago White Sox

YEAR	SS	TEAM
1960 NL	Ernie Banks	Chicago Cubs
1960 AL	Luis Aparicio	Chicago White Sox
1961 NL	Maury Wills	Los Angeles Dodgers
1961 AL	Luis Aparicio	Chicago White Sox
1962 NL	Maury Wills	Los Angeles Dodgers
1962 AL	Luis Aparicio	Chicago White Sox
1963 NL	Bobby Wine	Philadelphia Phillies
1963 AL	Zoilo Versalles	Minnesota Twins
1964 NL	Ruben Amaro	Philadelphia Phillies
1964 AL	Luis Aparicio	Baltimore Orioles
1965 NL	Leo Cardenas	Cincinnati Reds
1965 AL	Zoilo Versalles	Minnesota Twins
1966 NL	Gene Alley	Pittsburgh Pirates
1966 AL	Luis Aparicio	Baltimore Orioles
1967 NL	Gene Alley	Pittsburgh Pirates
1967 AL	Jim Fregosi	California Angels
1968 NL	Dal Maxvill	St. Louis Cardinals
1968 AL	Luis Aparicio	Chicago White Sox
1969 NL	Don Kessinger	Chicago Cubs
1969 AL	Mark Belanger	Baltimore Orioles
1970 NL	Don Kessinger	Chicago Cubs
1970 AL	Luis Aparicio	Chicago White Sox
1971 NL	Bud Harrelson	New York Mets
1971 AL	Mark Belanger	Baltimore Orioles
1972 NL	Larry Bowa	Philadelphia Phillies
1972 AL	Ed Brinkman	Detroit Tigers
1973 NL	Roger Metzger	Houston Astros
1973 AL	Mark Belanger	Baltimore Orioles
1974 NL	Dave Concepcion	Cincinnati Reds
1974 AL	Mark Belanger	Baltimore Orioles
1975 NL	Dave Concepcion	Cincinnati Reds
1975 AL	Mark Belanger	Baltimore Orioles
1976 NL	Dave Concepcion	Cincinnati Reds

Gold Glove Shortstops *(continued)*

YEAR	SS	TEAM
1976 AL	Mark Belanger	Baltimore Orioles
1977 NL	Dave Concepcion	Cincinnati Reds
1977 AL	Mark Belanger	Baltimore Orioles
1978 NL	Larry Bowa	Philadelphia Phillies
1978 AL	Mark Belanger	Baltimore Orioles
1979 NL	Dave Concepcion	Cincinnati Reds
1979 AL	Rick Burleson	Boston Red Sox
1980 NL	Ozzie Smith	San Diego Padres
1980 AL	Alan Trammell	Detroit Tigers
1981 NL	Ozzie Smith	San Diego Padres
1981 AL	Alan Trammell	Detroit Tigers
1982 NL	Ozzie Smith	St. Louis Cardinals
1982 AL	Robin Yount	Milwaukee Brewers
1983 NL	Ozzie Smith	St. Louis Cardinals
1983 AL	Alan Trammell	Detroit Tigers
1984 NL	Ozzie Smith	St. Louis Cardinals
1984 AL	Alan Trammell	Detroit Tigers
1985 NL	Ozzie Smith	St. Louis Cardinals
1985 AL	Alfredo Griffin	Oakland Athletics
1986 NL	Ozzie Smith	St. Louis Cardinals
1986 AL	Tony Fernandez	Toronto Blue Jays
1987 NL	Ozzie Smith	St. Louis Cardinals
1987 AL	Tony Fernandez	Toronto Blue Jays
1988 NL	Ozzie Smith	St. Louis Cardinals
1988 AL	Tony Fernandez	Toronto Blue Jays
1989 NL	Ozzie Smith	St. Louis Cardinals
1989 AL	Tony Fernandez	Toronto Blue Jays
1990 NL	Ozzie Smith	St. Louis Cardinals
1990 AL	Ozzie Guillen	Chicago White Sox
1991 NL	Ozzie Smith	St. Louis Cardinals
1991 AL	Cal Ripken Jr.	Baltimore Orioles

YEAR	SS	TEAM
1992 NL	Ozzie Smith	St. Louis Cardinals
1992 AL	Cal Ripken Jr.	Baltimore Orioles
1993 NL	Jay Bell	Pittsburgh Pirates
1993 AL	Omar Vizquel	Seattle Mariners
1994 NL	Barry Larkin	Cincinnati Reds
1994 AL	Omar Vizquel	Cleveland Indians
1995 NL	Barry Larkin	Cincinnati Reds
1995 AL	Omar Vizquel	Cleveland Indians
1996 NL	Barry Larkin	Cincinnati Reds
1996 AL	Omar Vizquel	Cleveland Indians
1997 NL	Rey Ordonez	New York Mets
1997 AL	Omar Vizquel	Cleveland Indians
1998 NL	Rey Ordonez	New York Mets
1998 AL	Omar Vizquel	Cleveland Indians
1999 NL	Rey Ordonez	New York Mets
1999 AL	Omar Vizquel	Cleveland Indians

CESAR IZTURIS

Gold Glove Shortstops *(continued)*

YEAR	SS	TEAM
2000 NL	Neifi Perez	Colorado Rockies
2000 AL	Omar Vizquel	Cleveland Indians
2001 NL	Orlando Cabrera	Montreal Expos
2001 AL	Omar Vizquel	Cleveland Indians
2002 NL	Edgar Renteria	St. Louis Cardinals
2002 AL	Alex Rodriguez	Texas Rangers
2003 NL	Edgar Renteria	St. Louis Cardinals
2003 AL	Alex Rodriguez	Texas Rangers
2004 NL	Cesar Izturis	Los Angeles Dodgers
2004 AL	Derek Jeter	New York Yankees
2005 AL	Omar Vizquel	San Francisco Giants
2005 AL	Derek Jeter	New York Yankees

Most Games Played at Shortstop

Luis Aparicio	2583	Roy McMillan	2028
Ozzie Smith	2511	Pee Wee Reese	2014
Cal Ripken Jr.	2302	Roger Peckinpaugh	1982
Omar Vizquel*	2275	Garry Templeton	1964
Larry Bowa	2222	Don Kessinger	1955
Luke Appling	2218	Mark Belanger	1942
Dave Concepcion	2178	Chris Speier	1900
Rabbit Maranville	2153	Ozzie Guillen	1896
Alan Trammell	2139	Honus Wagner	1887
Bill Dahlen	2132	Dick Groat	1877
Bert Campaneris	2097	Dave Bancroft	1873
Barry Larkin	2085	Donie Bush	1867
Tommy Corcoran	2073		

*still active

Rookie of the Year Shortstops

1948	ML	Alvin Dark, Boston Braves
1953	AL	Harvey Kuenn, Detroit Tigers
1956	AL	Luis Aparicio, Chicago White Sox

(Yes, we know that Tony Kubek won in 57, but
he played more games in the outfield)

1960	AL	Ron Hansen, Baltimore Orioles
1962	AL	Tom Tresh, New York Yankees
1979	AL	Alfredo Griffin, Toronto Blue Jays (tie)
1982	AL	Cal Ripken Jr., Baltimore Orioles
1985	AL	Ozzie Guillen, Chicago White Sox
1988	AL	Walt Weiss, Oakland A s
1992	AL	Pat Listach, Milwaukee Brewers
1996	AL	Derek Jeter, New York Yankees
1997	AL	Nomar Garciaparra, Boston Red Sox
2000	NL	Rafael Furcal, Atlanta Braves
2003	AL	Angel Berroa, Kansas City Royals
2004	AL	Bobby Crosby, Oakland A s

BOBBY CROSBY   **ANGEL BERROA**

Hall of Fame Shortstops
(only includes those elected as a player with most GP at short)

PLAYER	FROM-TO	IND	G	AB	R	H
Honus Wagner	1897-1917	1936	2792	10430	1736	3415
Hughie Jennings	1891-1918	1945	1285	4904	994	1527
Joe Tinker	1902-1916	1946	1804	6434	774	1687
Bobby Wallace	1894-1918	1953	2383	8618	1057	2309
Rabbit Maranville	1912-1935	1954	2670	10078	1255	2605
Joe Cronin	1926-1945	1956	2124	7579	1233	2285
Luke Appling	1930-1950	1964	2422	8856	1319	2749
John Ward	1878-1894	1964	1825	7647	1408	2104
Lou Boudreau	1938-1952	1970	1646	6029	861	1779
Dave Bancroft	1915-1930	1971	1913	7182	1048	2004
Joe Sewell	1920-1933	1977	1903	7132	1141	2226
Travis Jackson	1922-1936	1982	1656	6086	833	1768
Luis Aparicio	1956-1973	1984	2601	10230	1335	2677
Pee Wee Reese	1940-1958	1984	2166	8058	1338	2170
Arky Vaughan	1932-1948	1985	1817	6622	1173	2103
Phil Rizzuto	1941-1956	1994	1661	5816	877	1588
George Davis	1890-1909	1998	2368	9031	1539	2660
Robin Yount	1974-1993	1999	2856	11008	1632	3142
Ozzie Smith	1978-1996	2002	2573	9396	1257	2460

Transcendental Graphics

HONUS WAGNER

2B	3B	HR	RBI	BB	SO	BA	OBP	SLG	SB	CS	OPS+
640	252	101	1732	963	327	.327	.391	.466	722	15	150
232	88	18	840	347	117	.311	.390	.406	359	0	117
263	114	31	782	416	149	.262	.308	.353	336	0	96
391	143	34	1121	774	79	.268	.332	.358	201	2	105
380	177	28	884	839	756	.258	.318	.340	291	93	82
515	118	170	1424	1059	700	.301	.390	.468	87	71	119
440	102	45	1116	1302	528	.310	.399	.398	179	108	112
231	96	26	867	420	326	.275	.314	.341	540	0	93
385	66	68	789	796	309	.295	.380	.415	51	50	120
320	77	32	591	827	487	.279	.355	.358	145	75	98
436	68	49	1055	842	114	.312	.391	.413	74	72	109
291	86	135	929	412	565	.291	.337	.433	71	13	102
394	92	83	791	736	742	.262	.311	.343	506	136	82
330	80	126	885	1210	890	.269	.366	.377	232	45	99
356	128	96	926	937	276	.318	.406	.453	118	0	136
239	62	38	563	651	398	.273	.351	.355	149	58	93
451	163	73	1437	870	180	.295	.361	.405	616	0	121
583	126	251	1406	966	1350	.285	.342	.430	271	105	115
402	69	28	793	1072	589	.262	.337	.328	580	148	87

Single Game Shortstops since 1900

Andy Sullivan, Boston Beaneaters	1904
Joe Giannini, Boston Red Sox	1911
Vincent Maney, Detroit Tigers	1912
Charlie Miller, St. Louis Browns	1912
Al Cabrera, St. Louis Cardinals	1913
Monte Peffer, Philadelphia Athletics	1913
Billy Martin, Boston Braves	1914
Shorty Dee, St. Louis Browns	1915
Ed Murray, St. Louis Browns	1917
Otto Neu, St. Louis Browns	1917
Jesse Baker, Washington Senators	1919
Wally Dashiell, Chicago White Sox	1924
Frank Naleway, Chicago White Sox	1924
Frank Trechock, Washington Senators	1937
Tony Ordenana, Pittsburgh Pirates	1943
Frank Verdi, New York Yankees	1953
Chris Kitsos, Chicago Cubs	1954

Top Nine Shortstop Nicknames

Larvell "Sugar Bear" Blanks
Pompeyo Antonio "Yo-Yo" Davalillo
Leonard Norris "Bananas" Foster
Ewell "Turkey" Gross
Walter James Vincent "Rabbit" Maranville
Harold Henry "Pee Wee" Reese
"The Wizard of Oz" Osborne Earl Smith
Charles Ernest "Spider" Wilhelm
Orville Inman "Coot" Veal

All-Star Game MVP Shortstops

1962   Maury Wills, Los Angeles Dodgers (tie)
1982   Dave Concepcion, Cincinnati Reds
1991   Cal Ripken Jr., Baltimore Orioles
2000   Derek Jeter, New York Yankees
2001   Cal Ripken Jr., Baltimore Orioles
2005   Miguel Tejada, Baltimore Orioles

World Series MVP Shortstops

1978   Bucky Dent, New York Yankees
1984   Alan Trammell, Detroit Tigers
2000   Derek Jeter, New York Yankees

MIGUEL TEJADA   DEREK JETER

#1 Overall Shortstop Draft Picks

1968   Tim Foli, New York Mets
1974   Bill Almon, San Diego Padres
1982   Shawon Dunston, Chicago Cubs
1990   Chipper Jones, Atlanta Braves
1993   Alex Rodriguez, Seattle Mariners
2004   Matt Bush, San Diego Padres
2005   Justin Upton, Arizona Diamondbacks

Our Lineup

After *The Sporting News* selected him as their College Player of the Year, the San Diego Padres made **Bill Almon** the number one overall pick in the draft in 1974. The Padres had also drafted Almon out of high school three years earlier, but he decided to attend his hometown college, Brown University, making him one of the few Ivy League graduates to play in the major leagues. By 1977 Almon was the Padres' starting shortstop, but lost his job the following season to future Hall of Famer Ozzie Smith. For the rest of his career, including stints with the Expos, Mets, White Sox, A's, Pirates, and Phillies, Almon served as a utilityman, playing every position except for pitcher. In his 15-year career he appeared in 1,188 major league games, including 616 at short.

Larvell "Sugar Bear" Blanks played 9 major league seasons with Atlanta, Texas, and Cleveland after being drafted in the third round by the Braves in 1969. He started at short for the Braves in 1975, but after hitting a mere .234 was traded twice in a single day. On December 12 Atlanta sent Blanks to Chicago in a multi-player deal. The White Sox then traded Blanks to Cleveland, where he would spend the next three seasons. After playing in both the Mexican and Senior Professional Baseball Leagues, Blanks settled in Arizona where he is a junior high school teacher.

Bobby Bonner played alongside Cal Ripken Jr. in 1981 for the Triple A Rochester Red Wings. Together they took part in the longest game in professional baseball history, a 33-inning loss to Pawtucket. Bonner played short and went 3 for 13 while Ripken played third and went 2 for 13. Ripken's Pawtucket counterpart at third base, Wade Boggs, was 4 for 12 with a double and a RBI. Ripken and Bonner also share a 1982 Topps rookie card. Bonner appeared in 61 major league games for the Orioles from 1980-1983, including 50 at shortstop. After spending time as a missionary in Zambia, Bonner has returned to his native Texas where he is the CEO of I AM (International African Missions) Ministries.

Larry Bowa, a five-time All-Star and two-time Gold Glove Award winner, spent the majority of his 16-year playing career with the Philadelphia Phillies, including the 1980 season when the Phillies won the World Championship. Known as one of baseball's most fiery competitors, Bowa managed the San Diego Padres in 1987 and 1988 before returning to Philadelphia to manage from 2001-2004. He spent the 2005 as a broadcast analyst for ESPN and in 2006 will serve as third base coach for the New York Yankees. Bowa played 2,222 major league games at shortstop, ranking fifth on the all-time list.

South Carolina native **Don Buddin** signed with the Boston Red Sox as an amateur free agent in 1952 and joined the major league squad in 1956. He played five seasons with Boston before being traded to the expansion Houston Colt .45s. There he hit the first grand slam in franchise history on June 10, 1962, off Dodgers pitcher Joe Moeller, a game the .45s lost 9-7.

Although a Dodgers fan growing up, **Bruce Christensen** was drafted by his other hometown team, the California Angels, in the 17th round of baseball's second annual draft in 1966. The left-handed batter made his major league debut with the Angels on July 17, 1971, and played in 29 games in his only big league season. He retired with a lifetime batting average of .270 and a fielding percentage of .988. He lives in Moroni, Utah, where he is active in the Utah chapter of the Major League Baseball Alumni Association.

In 1982, his only year as a starting major league shortstop, **Mike Fischlin** hit .268, well above his career average, for the Cleveland Indians. Though selected by the New York Yankees in the seventh round of the 1975 draft and making the majors just two seasons later, it would be 1986, after stints with Houston and Cleveland, before Fischlin finally appeared in pinstripes. He also appeared in one game for the Atlanta Braves. The first client of famed sports agent Scott Boras, Fischlin lives outside Atlanta, where he serves as a Vice President for the Scott Boras Corporation.

Best known as the right-hand man of manager Sparky Anderson, **Alex Grammas** has viewed more games from the third base coaching box than any man in history. Grammas played 913 National League games for the Reds, Cardinals, and Cubs over a ten-season playing career lasting from 1954 to 1963. He resides in his hometown of Birmingham, Alabama.

In four years at Clemson University, **Khalil Greene** was a four-time All-ACC Academic honor roll selection and made two trips to the College World Series. Greene also holds Clemson career marks in hits, doubles, RBI, extra-base hits and total bases. His dominance on the collegiate playing field led the San Diego Padres to select Greene in the first round (13th overall) in 2002. By 2003 Greene had reached the majors, and he has held down the Padres' starting shortstop position for the last two seasons. In 2004 Greene finished second to the Pirates' Jason Bay in National League Rookie of the Year voting.

Dick Groat was a two-time All-American at Duke University in both baseball and basketball, and in 1952 he made both his major league and NBA debuts. A first-round draft pick of the Fort Wayne Pistons, Groat averaged 11.9 points per game in his only NBA season. That same year he played in 95 games with the Pittsburgh Pirates and held a .284 batting average. A five-time major league All-Star, Groat would bat .300 or better in four different seasons, including 1960 when his league-leading .325 average helped him win the National League MVP Award. Groat, who never played a single day in the minor leagues, was the starting shortstop for World Championship teams in 1960 and 1964.

Joe Koppe, the eleventh of fourteen children, was born in Detroit, Michigan, and grew up next door to Tigers shortstop Johnny Lipon. Koppe made his major league debut with the Milwaukee Braves in 1958, and by 1961 had made his way to Los Angeles, where he became the starting shortstop for the expansion Angels. He held that job for nearly two years until an ill-advised slide into the shin guards of Yogi Berra simultaneously knocked Koppe out of the lineup and opened up a spot for 20-year-old Jim Fregosi. Though he appeared in 128 games (including 118 at short) in 1962, after Fregosi's ascension Koppe played just 54 games at shortstop during his final three years in the majors.

A native of Buffalo, New York, **Jack Kubiszyn** was an All-SEC baseball and basketball player at the University of Alabama before signing with the Cleveland Indians in 1958. He made his major league debut as a pinch-runner against the Kansas City Athletics on April 23, 1961, and was called out trying to go from first to third on a Johnny Temple single. Cleveland won the game 10-8. Kubiszyn is the 13th player in major league history to have his first home run decide a 1-0 ballgame. It would be the only round-tripper of his career. A former junior college baseball coach and city councilman, Kubiszyn sells insurance in Tuscaloosa, Alabama.

One of just six major leaguers to attend St. Edward's University in Austin, Texas, (and the only player since 1945), **Roger Metzger** was the Cubs' number one draft pick in 1969, but appeared in just one game for Chicago before being traded to the Astros for Hector Torres. Metzger went on to play more games at short than any other man in Houston franchise history. He led the National League in triples in 1971 and 1973 and won the National League Gold Glove Award in '73. His worst on-field injury, a broken thumb, came from a pre-game warmup collision with pitcher Don Wilson. Metzger finished his 1,219 game major league career with the Giants in 1980. He lives in Brenham, Texas, where he works for the Department of Aging and Disabled Services.

South Amboy, New Jersey, natives and twin brothers Johnny and **Eddie O'Brien** attended Seattle University where they played both baseball and basketball. And though there were pro basketball offers, the brothers signed bonus contracts with Branch Rickey to play baseball for the Pittsburgh Pirates. On May 10, 1953, the O'Briens became the first twins to play for the same team in the same game. And though Eddie and Johnny were primarily middle infielders, the Pirates' acquisitions of Dick Groat and Bill Mazeroski eventually forced both brothers to the pitcher's mound. From 1956 to 1958 Eddie pitched 16 ⅓ major league innings and compiled a record of 1-0. After he retired as a player he served as athletic director and baseball coach at his alma mater, as well as serving a stint as a coach for the infamous 1969 Seattle Pilots.

Over his ten-year career **Desi Relaford** has worn six major league uniforms—the Phillies, Padres, Mets, Mariners, Royals, and Rockies. He was also a member of the San Francisco Giants for a little more than a month during the 2001/2002 off-season. Subsequent to his release by the Rockies in August of 2005, Relaford signed a minor league contract with an eighth organization, the Toronto Blue Jays. On top of over 450 games as a major league shortstop, Relaford has also played at least one game at every other position save for catcher and first base. He is also the owner of the hip/hop music label 6hole Records.

Though he didn't play his first major league game until September 17, 2000, (a game in which he went 2 for 4 with a walk, a triple, a stolen base and two runs scored), **Jimmy Rollins** is already a three-time National League All-Star shortstop. He led the league in at-bats in 2001 and 2002, as well as in triples in 2001, 2002, and 2004. A second round draft pick of the Phillies in 1996, Rollins finished the 2005 season with a 36-game hitting streak.

Texas native **Bart Shirley** signed a free agent contract with the Dodgers in 1961 and played three of his four major league seasons in Los Angeles. On August 8, 1968, he had the lone Los Angeles hit, a third-inning single, as Rick Wise shut out the Dodgers 1-0 thanks to a ninth-inning home run by Phillies slugger Dick Allen. Shirley retired from baseball after playing the 1972 season in Japan.

Along with Pete Runnels and Whitey Herzog, **Daryl Spencer** began his professional career in 1947 in Oklahoma's Center State League. One of the very few shortstop sluggers of his era, Spencer remains the only National League middle infielder to hit 20 home runs in his rookie season. Spencer also hit the first West Coast home run in major league history when he took Don Drysdale deep on Opening Day 1958. After ten major league seasons with the Giants, Dodgers, Cardinals, and Reds, Spencer played baseball in Japan and is purportedly the first ballplayer to physically break up a double play there.

In 1999 **Bill Spiers** was named by Sports Illustrated as one of South Carolina's 50 Greatest Sports Figures. At Clemson Spiers was not only a two-time all-conference baseball selection, but he also punted for coach Danny Ford's 1986 Gator Bowl team. Selected by the Milwaukee Brewers with the 13th overall pick in the 1987 draft, Spiers played 13 major league seasons, despite suffering a serious back injury during the Brewers' final home game in 1991. On October 1, 1998, Spiers' ninth-inning single against Padres closer Trevor Hoffman gave Houston its only win in the Division Series.

A graduate of Stanford University, **Paul Zuvella** played

parts of nine major league seasons after being drafted by Atlanta in the 15th round in 1980. In his first major league appearance with the Braves Zuvella also committed his first major league error. After cleanly fielding a grounder off the bat of future Hall of Famer Johnny Bench, Zuvella overthrew the second baseman covering for the force play. Following his playing career, Zuvella served as a minor league coach for six seasons. He now sells real estate in California's Bay Area.

ABOUT THE AUTHOR

John Marvosa

The author with Elrod Hendricks

Rob Trucks is on the thin side of handsome, a veritable pole vault stanchion of a man. He is the author of *Cup of Coffee: The Very Short Careers of Eighteen Major League Pitchers* (Smallmouth Press, 2003), *The Pleasure of Influence: Conversations with American Male Fiction Writers* (Purdue University Press, 2002) as well as the first two titles in the *Baseball Behind The Seams* series, *The Catcher* and *The Starting Pitcher* (Emmis Books, 2005). Trucks writes about baseball, music, and literature for *Spin, No Depression, BookForum, East Bay Express, Philadelphia Weekly, Cleveland Scene, Baltimore City Paper, Boulder Weekly,* and *Phoenix New Times,* among other publications, from his closet-sized apartment in Long Island City, New York, but longs to move to Albany so he can truthfully call himself an Albanian.

Books of Interest

Baseball Behind the Seams

The **Baseball Behind the Seams** series presents baseball the way it ought to be: no pouting superstars, no steroids, no players' strikes. Each book in this one-of-a-kind series focuses on a single position, exploring it with the kind of depth serious fans crave. Through extensive research, including interviews with hundreds of players past and present, the authors have brought together the most original and informative series ever published on the game.

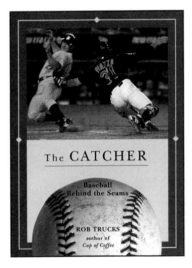

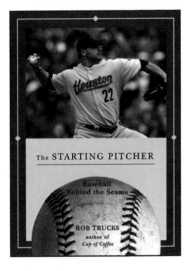

The Catcher
By Rob Trucks
$14.99 Paperback
ISBN: 1-57860-164-9

The Starting Pitcher
By Rob Trucks
$14.99 Paperback
ISBN: 1-57860-163-0

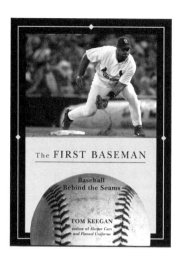

The First Baseman
By Tom Keegan
$14.95 Paperback
ISBN: 1-57860-261-0

Each book in the series covers
- The physical and mental qualities of the position
- The position's history
- The plays, and how to make them
- Profiles of the position's top all-time players
- The best defenders of the position
- A day in the life of one player, from arriving at the ballpark to the final out
- Lists of Gold Glovers, MVPs, and Rookies of the Year
- Fun and quirky facts about the position